The Ethics of Silence

Nancy Billias • Sivaram Vemuri

The Ethics of Silence

An Interdisciplinary Case Analysis Approach

Nancy Billias
University of Saint Joseph
West Hartford, Connecticut, USA

Sivaram Vemuri
Charles Darwin University
Darwin, Australia

ISBN 978-3-319-84386-5   ISBN 978-3-319-50382-0 (eBook)
DOI 10.1007/978-3-319-50382-0

© The Editor(s) (if applicable) and The Author(s) 2017
Softcover reprint of the hardcover 1st edition 2017
This work is subject to copyright. All rights are solely and exclusively licensed by the Publisher, whether the whole or part of the material is concerned, specifically the rights of translation, reprinting, reuse of illustrations, recitation, broadcasting, reproduction on microfilms or in any other physical way, and transmission or information storage and retrieval, electronic adaptation, computer software, or by similar or dissimilar methodology now known or hereafter developed.
The use of general descriptive names, registered names, trademarks, service marks, etc. in this publication does not imply, even in the absence of a specific statement, that such names are exempt from the relevant protective laws and regulations and therefore free for general use.
The publisher, the authors and the editors are safe to assume that the advice and information in this book are believed to be true and accurate at the date of publication. Neither the publisher nor the authors or the editors give a warranty, express or implied, with respect to the material contained herein or for any errors or omissions that may have been made. The publisher remains neutral with regard to jurisdictional claims in published maps and institutional affiliations.

Cover illustration: PhotoAlto / Alamy Stock Photo

Printed on acid-free paper

This Palgrave Macmillan imprint is published by Springer Nature
The registered company is Springer International Publishing AG
The registered company address is: Gewerbestrasse 11, 6330 Cham, Switzerland

"To our teachers, our students, and our colleagues, with love and gratitude"

Preface

This little book began as a conversation between two friends from very different disciplines and backgrounds who were each sincerely searching for some small way to make the world a more ethical place. Each of us had, independently, become fascinated with the topic of silence. The dialogue between the two of us has expanded into a global conversation with people from several continents and disciplines. And it is only just beginning.

We realize that we have only barely scratched the surface of the topic at hand. Our goal was not to be prescriptive about how silence should be understood and managed, but rather to put forward some suggestions for consideration, and invite you, the reader, to contemplate how silence appears in your own context, and how you might employ some of the ideas in this volume in the pursuit of more reflective – rather than reflexive – action. The case studies presented here provide illustrations and examples of people doing just that. We hope that as you read this book, you will begin to imagine how you might interpret and implement these ideas in your own particular context.

This is not intended to be a book for academics: certainly not for professional philosophers or economists. Excellent books of that genre already exist in the fields of art, science, and the humanities. Our intention, rather, was to write for those beyond the ivory towers of academia, for people in any walk of life, facing the ethical dilemmas of living and working in the twenty-first century. Thus we have tried as best we can to steer clear of disciplinary jargon and a "high" academic tone. We hope that our research will stimulate both reflection and discussion. Perhaps paradoxically, we hope that this book will give you some ideas on how to manage silence in order to improve communication.

As is customary in academia today, we have made every effort to use gender-neutral language throughout this volume. In order to do so, we sometimes alternate between female and male pronouns when using a single individual as an example of common practice.

The material that appears in quotation marks in each chapter is taken from interviews conducted by the researchers jointly via Skype, between December 2014 and August 2016. The method of working was as follows:

1. After an initial request for interview, the respondent was sent an Institutional Review Board form to sign, indicating consent for publication of his/her words, in line with standard social science research protocol.
2. We sent minimal background information about the project, as we did not want respondents to tailor their answers to preconceived ideas. We simply told them that we were investigating how silence is manifested across different cultures and in different social situations, especially with regard to decision-making.
3. During the Skype interviews, Prof. Vemuri took the lead in posing questions, while Prof. Billias typed a verbatim transcript. We began each interview by asking for a brief biographical sketch and for some information regarding the context of the fieldwork.
4. After the interview, Prof. Billias refined the transcript to omit typographical/grammatical errors. Then after a period of reflection on the text, we began the case analysis.
5. Upon completion of the analysis, a draft of the chapter was sent back to the respondents. We asked them to ensure that we had captured their experience accurately, and that we had neither added anything, nor taken anything away from what they wished to express. This feedback was then incorporated into the final version of that chapter.

We would like to thank the many people who helped bring this book to the light of day. First and foremost, we are extremely grateful to our respondents, who gave so generously their time and expertise, both in participating in the interviews and in reviewing our analyses of their cases. We have learned a great deal through this process, both about silence and about interdisciplinarity.

List of Interviewees

Vivian Carlson, PhD, is Professor Emerita of Human Development and Family Studies at the University of Saint Joseph, West Hartford, Connecticut, USA. She spends up to two months each year in Guyana providing humanitarian services to the Amerindian peoples of the Rupununi.

Jarrett Davis, MA, is a field researcher for the anti-trafficking organization Love146. He is currently stationed in Phnom Penh, Cambodia.

Julian Gorman, PhD, is a Research Fellow of the Research Institute for the Environment and Livelihoods at Charles Darwin University, Darwin, Northern Territory, Australia.

Jasmine Mendiola, MA, is the Assistant Director of the Marine and Environmental Research Institute of the Pacific in Pohnpei, Micronesia.

Samite Mulondo is a world musician, composer, humanitarian worker, and photographer. He is the founder of the NGO Musicians for World Harmony.

Herb Ruffin II, PhD, is Associate Professor and Chair of the Department of African American Studies at Syracuse University, Syracuse, New York, USA.

Cristina Santos, PhD, is Associate Professor of Hispanic and Latin American Studies at Brock University in St. Catharine's, Ontario.

Ela Wysakowski Walters, MFA, is a freelance visual and inter-media artist and translator based in Kuczki, Poland. Her artwork has been exhibited in Germany, Poland, the United States, and Venezuela.

Special gratitude is due to Rob Fisher, Founder and Network Leader of Inter-Disciplinary.Net, Oxford, United Kingdom. The authors would never have encountered one another had it not been for his energetic and creative vision in hosting global interdisciplinary conferences.

Our gratitude goes also to Jonathan Gourlay, of the University of Saint Joseph in West Hartford, Connecticut, and especially to Sean Moran, of the Waterford Institute of Technology in Tipperaray, Ireland, who patiently read drafts of various chapters, and to Edward Emery, for his wise counsel and guidance at the outset of the project. This book is much stronger and clearer as a result of your input.

We would also like to thank our families, especially Jyoti Vemuri, for putting up with our intermittent silence whilst we were engaged in this project. We could not have completed this work without your patience, love, and understanding.

Contents

1 Introduction — 1

2 Working with Silence — 17

3 Whose Silence? Hearing Echoes of Disembodied Trauma (Argentina) — 35

4 Silence Looking Out and Looking In (Southeast Asia) — 47

5 The Silence of the Unknown and the Unknowable (Guyana) — 67

6 How Many Layers of Silence Can One Context Hold? (Micronesia) — 79

7 Who May Speak? Who Must Be Silent? (Australia) — 93

8 Individual, Collective, and Strategic Silences (USA) — 107

9 Visible Silence (Poland/Germany) — 131

10	The Healing Qualities of Silence (Uganda)	147
11	Reflections	161

Index 177

CHAPTER 1

Introduction

The Importance of Silence in Communication

Silence is an essential and ubiquitous aspect of all communication. In order to explore the topic adequately – and clarify its importance to ethics – an interdisciplinary approach is necessary. In this instance, the authors draw upon the methodologies of economics and philosophy, as well as the expertise of practitioners in different areas of fieldwork. The task is to understand the various modalities of silence as they emerge in a variety of social contexts that bring together people with divergent needs, histories, and power bases. How is silence currently used in decision-making processes, at macro- and micro-levels? How is silence understood by the different parties involved? What are the effects of silence and the implications entailed in each modality? Finally, and most importantly, how can these various aspects of silence be reimagined to promote social transformation?

Defining silence is not easy. Silence is too complex a phenomenon to be defined in a prescriptive manner. It is therefore best understood by describing certain of its salient features. Silence means different things to different people. It is only observable if one pays attention to it; otherwise it is largely ignored. The present book grew out of a mutual concern relating to the ethical issues impacting upon decision-making in the world today. As academics and practitioners, we recognize that the world is becoming ever noisier. Many have lamented elsewhere that the technology which has enabled instant communication throughout the world has also increased social isolation, voter apathy, hardening of extreme viewpoints, and the siloing of information.

Silence is more than the lack of an auditory signal. It is also very different from other forms of communication. Therefore it is more than a communication metaphor. Silence is omnipresent. It permeates all contexts and situations, although many do not realize its existence, importance, and power of influence. For example, at the level of the individual and the family, as well as societally, one is surrounded by silence. But often silence is not noticed until it is too late.

The intrinsic character of silence is that its presence can only be felt by those who possess an ability to observe, analyze, and comprehend, and are open-minded about opinions and alternative views to their own. Silence can play an important role in addressing contemporary issues of concern, by enabling the development and inclusion of alternative points of view and promoting pluralistic values.

Silence is powerful. When not expressed, feelings and thoughts can build up an internal pressure, whether on the part of an individual or between members of a couple, family, or group. Such pressure might lead to depression, resentment, and anger, which can manifest as self-harm, family breakups due to work-life imbalances, domestic violence, or even suicide. On the societal level, if one's voice is not heard and recognized – and if what one says is ignored or not incorporated into the decision-making process – further social dysfunction ensues. This can include the creation of bubbles and enclaves of minorities, an ever-growing inequality of contribution by individuals, and increasing levels of social stress and anxiety. The opposite of silence is the final scream of the suicide bomber. Paying more attention to silence might prevent the eruptions of frustration that leads to aggression, violence, and ultimately, to terrorism. We feel that a better "management" of silence is an ethical and hopeful way forward. There is more to management than "being managed." It requires reading the other – the one being managed. The ethical way forward that we envision involves being aware that managers intrude, disturb, and even command that notice is taken of the actions being solicited by those who are being managed. To achieve a new and more ethical outcome, we suggest that opportunities be provided for all points of view to be expressed in an atmosphere of suspended judgment. There will always be people who choose to be silent, and this their prerogative. Our purpose here is to open discussion, not to prescribe its shape.

Silence can also be used as a strategy to silence voices. There is a need to distinguish between silence and those who are silenced. An inscription on the Holocaust Memorial in Boston speaks of silence in the context of people in concentration camps of Nazi Germany – "Are you not listening to my screams for help? Why are you so silent?" Individuals have always been silenced by the forces of oppression, and mainstream society has often kept silent about individuals who were silenced. Both historically and in contemporary society, examples of these forms of atrocities are widespread. It is easy for the mainstream to impose its voice onto others. But where is the individual, when this occurs? This is, first and foremost, an ethical question. The ethics of silence implies, at the very least, that one leave room for the other, in which the other can be heard. But that is only the beginning of an answer.

The Need for an Interdisciplinary Approach

The study of diversity of silence in form, structure, and complexity merits an approach beyond the confines of narrow disciplinary boundaries. It warrants an interdisciplinary approach. We are distinguishing here between two forms of interdisciplinarity: weak and strong.

Weak interdisciplinarity is academically orientated, but goes beyond the reaches of one discipline. Theoretically, the disciplines and methodologies of economics and philosophy are both used as the basis for making ethical decisions. Both have unintended consequences in the real world. Each discipline, on its own, is inadequate. The impacts on mainstream society of individual disciplines attempting to deal with contemporary issues seem to be that matters are made worse. Part of the problem is that each discipline is highly selective – thus creating limitations on both the view of an issue and strategies that might be used to encourage meaningful change. Reality is complex and cannot be compartmentalized into disciplinary boundaries and perspectives. Thus, much information is lost or ignored; even in the process of inquiry itself.

Strong interdisciplinarity goes beyond academic discourse and is grounded in the contexts of lived reality. Because silence is all-pervasive, we could have chosen from a myriad of problems in applied ethics. We selected a few cases through which to discuss the significance and impact of silence in decision-making. We are looking at these cases through the perspectives of practitioners in terms of the reality of the dynamics involved, their observations and interpretations of what occurred, and possible suggestions toward meaningful social change. Our first undertaking is to discern the centrality of silence in communication and decision-making.

The fundamental prerequisite for communication and understanding is attention. The act of attention is the beginning of ethical behavior because it is through paying attention to the other that I move beyond myself into the space between us. The problem of linking the individual and a society, the regions within a nation, and nations with other nations globally, all require attention – perhaps today more urgently than ever before. Thus the act of attention is important for understanding the in-between space. Attending to the details is essential for any analysis of silence. These in-between spaces are filled with silences: different modalities of silence exist, largely dependent upon the processes used when individuals come together to form groups. A common feature amongst all these modalities of silence is that it is only possible to understand them when one moves beyond oneself.

The move beyond myself into the "space between us" can be achieved through a process of either infusion or diffusion. In the former, the initiation and direction of the process originates from the individual towards the group. The latter is a result of movement from the group towards the individual. Although the two processes – infusion and diffusion – contain all of the modalities of silence, different modalities are prominent in the various processes. An illustration of each of the processes from a contemporary context is provided here.

The process of infusion can be seen clearly in the case of diasporic communities which have gained increasing attention due to mass global migration. Today, one out of every five people was born in a place other than where he or she currently resides. So the concept of "what is it to be an individual in the global context" is coming under greater scrutiny than ever before. An individual is identified, amongst other criteria, on the basis of the ethnicity of a group to which she belongs. Individual migrants become members of diasporic communities by moving beyond themselves or being forced to make such a move by society. The space beyond the immigrant individual is filled through movement into the space between herself and the group. This is what we will refer as the "in-between spaces."

Often, individuals think that they freely choose to be a part of the membership of a diasporic community. But in reality, the underlying conditions that the individual faces in the place of the past (the country of origin) and the present (the country of residence) demand that the individual chooses to belong. No matter where she considers she belongs, she has moved from being an individual to becoming a member of a community. Infusion occurs as migrant individuals move into these in-between spaces. That process of movement is full of silence.

A different kind of dynamic is at work when analyzing silence as it relates to the process of diffusion. In this process, an in-between space is created when groups become individualistic in their orientation. For example, in discussions about indigenous economic development, the starting point for consideration is often the group and not the individual. In such cases, the act of attention needs to move beyond the group and toward the individual. A focus on the individual dominates contemporary thinking in every aspect of life. In the context of work with indigenous peoples, most consider chances of individual economic betterment to be hindered by vested interest groups (clans, tribes, and the like). Developmental advocates predominantly consider that group features stifle economic progress, and hence promote dispersal of groups into individuals. Those who pay attention can observe silence during the process of diffusion.

In these cases, the act of attention makes silence visible, and seeing it enables one to identify the different modalities of silence. In turn, the act of recognizing that silence exists in the processes both of diffusion and infusion makes ethics realizable. One can observe the presence and impact of silence by paying attention to the details of these activities – the movement, for example, from one scale of existence to another, as well as the movement from being to becoming – and being alert to the movements from one level of attention to the other – one can observe silence.

The Process and Role of Attention

Attention is not passive, but active and creative. Through the act of attention, I create meaning, both internally and in the world of others. Attention is active in two ways: it can be proactive or reactive. It also inscribes meanings – please note the plural – both internally and externally to the individual. Often it is in the creation of these meanings that misunderstanding occurs. In part, misunderstandings arise because the creation of a group is an extension of the past, and that past is used for interpreting the present and imagining the future. History becomes definitive.

For example, in the case of diasporic communities, people's reasons for migration and their ensuing migrant experiences are never the same. By paying attention to the uniqueness of these individual experiences, those involved create meanings for their own actions. In addition, the meanings of others' actions can be constructed. Meanings are assigned, interactions are interpreted with reference to the ascribed meanings, and opinions about oneself and others are formed and consolidated.

In the case of Indigenous Australia, past treatment (for instance the "stolen generation" of children, the governmental policy of eradication of indigenous languages, etc.) all play a very influential role in current discussions about education policies. The past becomes deterministic in the initial stages by ascribing meaning regarding how one creates an imagined self and interaction with "others." As greater attention is paid to historical experiences, redefining the meanings and interactions between internal and external forces can unleash change.

Attention begins at the thresholds of consciousness and intersubjectivity. The thresholds between consciousness and intersubjectivity provide a platform for focusing on "issues" and assists in conceptualizing "problems." As we traverse these thresholds, we transform issues into areas of concern. In so defining the problem, we are involved in a way of thinking about such concerns. The definition locks us into a way of thinking. Thus, we move from an abstract concept toward a living process, interacting with the other subjects with whom we are confronted.

Take, for a moment, the case of diasporic communities. The consciousness of being a member of a diaspora may entail an internal conflict at the threshold of consciousness, at the very point when one is feeling one's way toward acting as a subject. How can one identify as a member of an ethnic group (in a diaspora) when one may have been forcibly displaced from that group? For example, is a German Jew no longer a German? This dilemma of identification may be a silent conflict within the individual. In essence, the challenge the individual faces through consciousness and intersubjectivity is to answer the question: "Who am I"? Am I a hyphenated individual like the "Asian- American"? Or is my identity encapsulated by the descriptor "Registered Alien"? In either case, how do I act? As whom do I act? On whose behalf? Who am I?

In the case of indigenous peoples, a similar conflict of identity occurs at the thresholds of consciousness and intersubjectivity. Here the emphasis is also on ethnicity, but the focus is on the group rather than the individual. Just as the poor are blamed for being poor, Indigenous persons are blamed for being Indigenous. They wish to uphold their cultural values as a group, but in so doing, they face the allegation that this stifles economic progress. They maintain traditional mindsets in terms of contexts which no longer exist. By focusing on the group rather than the individual, the issue of identity becomes an obstacle for action.

Silence, Space, and Intersubjectivity

Silence is essential and integral to the act of attention. What we are seeking to do here is to outline the process and the means by which individuals establish themselves as ethical agents. Attention plays a key role in the construction of a self, both in terms of action and in terms of meaning-making. It is ethical action that establishes the world as real to the individual, and simultaneously establishes the individual as real within a social context. Ethical action defines the person, both within the self and in the community of others. Ethical action is the means by which the individual becomes real (to herself and others), makes the world real (to herself and others), and the means by which meaning is bestowed, both on the individual and on the world.

Internal silence is the space in which something new can emerge. Comprehension of internal silence cannot be undertaken in a vacuum. If I am to emerge into full-fledged consciousness, this must occur by means of the impetus of that context which stimulates "me" to move into an exploration of how I can expand meaning. In this schema, otherness is necessary to my development in and of meaning. It is not enough for me to bestow meanings on my actions, to articulate (to myself) a sense of significance. Meaning must also be ratified by the recognition of what is not-me: the other. What is felt is experienced and given significance within the context of that otherness. Otherwise, the event would have no transcendent quality, and no possibility of founding meaning; I would merely spin in concentric, solipsistic circles of sameness.

This intersubjective schema – the creation of myself through the other – has been well traced in Western philosophy, from Fichte to Hegel to Levinas. Simone Weil suggests that true attention

> consists of suspending our thought, leaving it detached, empty, and ready to be penetrated by the object; it means holding in our minds, within reach of this thought, but on a lower level and not in contact with it, the diverse knowledge we have acquired which we are forced to make use of. Our

thought should be in relation to all particular and already formulated thoughts, as a man on a mountain who, as he looks forward, sees also below him, without actually looking at them, a great many forests and plains.[1]

In the process of these "transactions," the individual creates herself, invents meaning, and then projects that meaning out into the world. As she chooses among actions, she seeks to justify her behavior intersubjectively. It is in this first moment of choice that the individual begins to take shape, and so, her world. Elsewhere, Weil goes even further, stating that "extreme attention is what constitutes the creative faculty in man."[2]

This reflective, attentive silence is the moment between decision and implementation. It is full of virtualities and potentialities. In this moment of creation, human freedom is born: both my freedom and the freedom of the other. This moment of freedom is the moment at which an ethics can emerge. This point can be identified with the moment of attention.

In the moment just prior to action, I am at my most free. At that liminal point, I have not yet entered – though I may be aware of – any causal chain. I may also be aware of difference. In fact, I must have such awareness, or what impetus would I have to take action? Yet the moment of attention is one in which I am not bound by difference, but rather can observe it without feeling caught up into it. Here again, Weil's understanding of attention comes to mind. In *Waiting for God*, she writes: "Above all our thought should be empty, waiting, not seeking anything, but ready to receive in its naked truth the object that is to penetrate it."[3]

The moment of attention holds the "virtualities" of responsibility, freedom, and agency. This moment is "moral" because it is the cradle of intersubjectivity: who I am in relation to the other(s). For even if I am on a determined or determining path – or find myself somewhere along a causal chain – each time I act, I can change the shape of my moral self in any one of a myriad of ways, and emerge from that action as a new being. At the same time, it is in "the pause at the crest of the breath", as Rilke puts it,

---

[1] Simone Weil, *Waiting on God*, 159.

[2] Weil anticipated this onto poietic understanding. In the essay "Attention and Will", Weil says: "Extreme attention is what constitutes the creative faculty in man." In *Gravity and Grace*, 170.

[3] Ibid., 111 ff.

that I can act toward the other in total freedom. At the moment prior to decision, I am – more properly said, I can be – free: of desire, will, reason, the demands of intersubjectivity, the burdens of self and other. I can float freely in the moment.

The French philosopher Emmanuel Levinas suggests that it is at the moment of the "interruption" of the self by the other – when the individual first becomes aware of the other – that the individual is revealed to itself for the first time, both ontologically (in terms of being) and ethically. It is here, Levinas claims, that we recognize – in the moment of awakening into the knowledge of our need for the other – our need to open a space for the other in which we can take our first breath as a true subject. This moment is eternally before us: it precedes and makes possible our being, both our being with others and our being as a self. The first moment, however, is a holding back, a moment of differentiation, and simultaneously a driving force for further action and analysis.

> In me – in the ego that yields [to the other], that renounces the right-of-way – life... holds its breath, its vitality as a "driving force."[4]

"Life holds its breath." It is only in this first moment of differentiation that the self is free of intersubjectivity, while it still floats in the space between the demands of the ego and the demands of the problems and issues of the individuals' lived context.

This moment can be called ethical in several ways. Firstly, because it gives birth to the ethical agent, the subject who can then choose to act. Secondly, because as a moment of absolute freedom it is the ideal starting point for an ethics. Thirdly, it is a moment that is saturated with responsibility, for, as Levinas (1998) reminds us, "every responsibility exists prior to freedom".[5] Because we know that in fact no action takes place in a vacuum, unrelated either to a history or a future. The moment prior to decision already holds within itself the responsibility for an ethical outcome. Will our action be ethically positive or negative? Will it contribute to greater harmony, or greater division between people? Will it move toward greater meaning, or away from meaning? The moment may be neutral, but of course the subsequent action is not.

---

[4] Emmanuel Levinas, *Ethics and Infinity*, 89.
[5] Ibid., 106.

A similar treatment of this problem can be found in the work of another thinker who was contemporaneous with Levinas: Karol Wojtyla, better known as Pope John Paul II. In his doctoral dissertation, *The Acting Person*, he writes:

> Consciousness is the "ground" on which the ego manifests itself in all its peculiar objectiveness (being the object of self-knowledge) and at the same time fully experiences its own subjectivity... the tasks of consciousness do not end with its illuminative and reflecting function... in fact, the essential function of consciousness is to form man's experience.[6]

That is, in consciousness, the person moves beyond reacting to her environment and towards what might be termed "real" or "authentic" action; action, that is, that may bear meaning. Consciousness allows us to "experience these actions as actions and as our own".[7]

This consciousness is the origin and first act of freedom, and opens the way for the creation of the person as agent. Wojtyla identifies free will with self-determination, and with transcendence:

> with the self-determination we discover the will as a constitutive element of the personal structure of man. Freedom thus manifests itself as connected with the will, with the concrete "I will," which includes... the experience of "I may but I need not."... The freedom appropriate to the human being, the person's freedom resulting from the will, exhibits itself as identical with self-determination, with that experiential, most complete, and fundamental organ of man's autonomous being. We are thus considering freedom as real, the freedom that constitutes the real and privileged position of man in the world and also the main condition of his will.[8]

"This premise is of essential significance", he continues. For Wojtyla, as for Levinas, the freedom thus manifested is the essential characteristic of human beings, that which results in the personal and the ethical. Acting means acting with others, participating in society and integrating the self and its needs with those of society. In so doing, the person transcends both solipsism and existential isolation.

---

[6] Karol Wojtyla, *The Acting* Person, 42.
[7] Loc. cit.
[8] Ibid., 115.

The root of this transcendence, which allows me to act as a self in relation to the other, can be found in the free moment of attention prior to action. Interestingly, this attention is not conscious: the attention at issue here is pre-reflective, pre-rational, and at the threshold of rationality. For reflection (at least according to Kant) is a function of the faculty of reason, and as such is always going to be in the service of the self, and speaking from the perspective of the self. Thus, reflection is always already, in one powerful sense, not free: not free of the consciousness of the self in a world of others. It is always already caught, created, and constructed within a social frame.

By contrast, listen to what Simone Weil thinks of the activity of attention:

> Thought, as we ordinarily understand it, is not quite the word...for thought implies the very focus that is intentionally suspended in this description of attention. At issue is the distinction between fastening the attention around a single phenomenon and leaving the attention open, a difference immediately understood by Weil in terms of larger freedoms and constraints: "If one desires a particular thing one becomes enslaved to the series of conditions. But if one desires the series itself, the satisfaction of this desire is unconditioned."[9]

Perhaps attention inhabits a pre-reflective space, a space in which the distinction between self and other is still more fluid than fixed. Attention can be understood as the origin of ethical action and the moral sense, for two reasons. Firstly, as a neutral and free starting point, attention is a most positive and hopeful point of departure. Secondly, it is conceivable that self-consciousness emerges from attention, as a simultaneous awareness of differentiation *from* the other and responsibility *for* the other.

If that is so, then, consciousness is in fact the resultant condition of attention. Further, the more this condition can be inhabited or cultivated, the greater the potential for meaning-giving will be enhanced. Attention could thus be truly understood as the birth of the individual as a subject in

---

[9] Sharon Cameron, "The Practice of Attention: Simone Weil's Performance of Impersonality," *Critical Inquiry*, 29:2 (Winter, 2003). Citation is from *Gravity and Grace*, 143.

the world of other subjects. From this perspective, then, we can begin to speak about a specifically human dignity.

Focusing on attention resolves the paradox between subjectivity as a matter of bondage, and subjectivity as the condition of free and meaningful interaction. The notion of attention allows us to move beyond intention – beyond mere intersubjectivity – and towards the infinite: the infinite space that exists between individual persons.[10]

This distance, this infinitude, can never be grasped by reason. It is beyond reason, unreasonable. Yet we apprehend it. It is a space which can only be approached, grasped, and attuned to by attention. Attention is mere vigilance; it is a form of being present with the other who is both infinitely close to me and infinitely distant from me, the neighbor whom I must love as myself, the other who calls to me out of sameness and whose call I must (and can never fully) answer. In this way, attention opens out/into infinity:

> The negativity of the In- of the Infinite...hollows out a desire that could not be filled, one nourished from its own increase...This is a Desire for what is beyond satisfaction, and which does not identify, as need does, a term or an end.[11]

ATTENTION AND ETHICS

While preceding subjectivity per se, attention opens the space for ethics. This is the space of responsibility which Levinas says always precedes freedom, and so human dignity, and so ethics. As the psychoanalyst Edward Emery remarks:

---

[10] I'm reminded here of one of Rilke's *Sonnets to Orpheus:* "How vast the distances between the stars; but we lie even farther apart/from each other. Stand one child next to a second, and see/between – how inconceivably far." From Sonnet II, 20: "Zwischen den Sternen, wie weit; und doch, um wievieles noch weiter, was man am Hiesigen lernt.Einer, zum Beispiel, ein Kind...und ein Nächster, ein Zweiter –, o wie unfässlich entfernt."

[11] Emmanuel Levinas, *Otherwise than Being,*, 67. See also Weil, *Gravity and Grace*, 171 ff:"Attention alone, that attention which is so full that the I disappears, is required of me. I have to deprive all that I call 'I' of the light of my attention and turn it onto that which cannot be conceived."

The bearing and crossing of this distance that can never reach destination or closure is the responsibility to which the infinite calls us.[12]

In this world of others, we are always already in the midst of a journey across this impossible, inconceivable void between self and other.

But what has all this to do with attention? Much ink has been spilled in the religious, philosophical, psychotherapeutic and sociological literature detailing the need for greater attentiveness to the other as the foundation of mindful action and compassion. Our purpose here is perhaps only slightly different: we want to focus on the effects of the phenomenon of attention not on the one to whom attention is paid, but on the one who pays attention. What does the act of attention engender in the self? More directly: what role does attention play in engendering the *self*? How is attention to be understood as creative – as chosen, as a substantively new and moral action, rather than merely as a response, no matter how positive?

The psychoanalyst Donald Winnicott observed hundreds of children in over 40 years of clinical work. In an essay written in 1941, Winnicott noted a behavioral pattern that is strikingly pertinent to our question. In observing very young infants (between 5 and 13 months old), he marked three distinct stages of attraction and attention to objects. (At this very early age, Winnicott feels, one's personality is extremely fluid.) In Winnicott's experience, the infant experiences confusion and conflict when wishes and fears emerge in the context of relationship with others. In the first stage, when presented with a new object, the child enters what Winnicott calls "the period of hesitation." During this time,

> the baby puts his hand to the [object], but at this moment discovers unexpectedly that the situation must be given thought. He is in a fix. Either with his hand resting on the [object] and his body quite still he looks at me and at his mother... and watches and waits, or in certain cases, he withdraws interest completely [and exhibits fear]... all this time... the

---

[12] Edward Emery, "Facing "O": Wilfred Bion, Emmanuel Levinas, and the Face of the Other (paper presented at "Face to Face with the Real World: Contemporary Applications of Levinas." March 17–19, 1999, Walsh University, Canton, Ohio and at the Ontario Institute for Studies in Education, University of Toronto, in conjunction with the Toronto Institute for Contemporary Psychoanalysis, May 22, 1999). Available at www.psychematters.com/papers/emery1.htm.

baby holds his body still (but not rigid). Gradually he becomes brave enough to let his feelings develop, and then the picture changes quite quickly. The moment at which this first phase changes into the second is evident, for the child's acceptance of the reality of desire for the [object] is heralded by [certain physiological changes]... The change in the baby's behavior is a striking feature. Instead of expectancy and stillness there now develops self-confidence, and there is free bodily movement... related to manipulation of the [object].[13]

Winnicott interprets this hesitation as the moment which gives rise both to desire and its accompanying anxieties – as the child begins to realize that her action will have both intentional and unintentional consequences. That is, the hesitation is the moment just before an engagement with the other, and a realization of responsibility.

The "something" which the anxiety is about is in the infant's mind, an idea of potential evil or strictness, and into the novel situation anything that is in the infant's mind may be projected. When there has been no experience of prohibition, the hesitation implies conflict, or the existence in the baby's mind of a fantasy corresponding to the... baby's memory of his really strict mother... these fantasies of the infant are concerned not only with external environment, but also with the fate and interrelationship of the people... that build up the inner reality.[14]

In other words, hesitation ends when consciousness of the self overagainst others begins, as part of our inner reality, and at the threshold of intersubjectivity. We suggest that one helpful way to begin grounding an ethics would be somehow to relocate and reclaim this moment of hesitation and attention. Perhaps attention can deliver us from the stranglehold of the ego into a more hopeful future, in which anxiety about desire and evil can be replaced by an integrated and integrative sense of unity. That is, maybe attention can help us to hold the doors of possibility open, instead of constantly foreclosing opportunities for intersubjective engagement.

---

[13] Donald Winnicott, "The Observation of Infants in a Set Situation", in *Through Pediatrics to Psychoanalysis: Collected Papers*, 53 ff. Our thanks to Dr. Edward Emery for bringing this case to our attention.

[14] Ibid., 55.

Perhaps in this way we might be able to realize Levinas' dream of responding to the other in a way that engenders freedom.

We end this introduction with a Zen ko'an which illustrates what we have been trying to say here.

> A student spends years gathering the resources necessary to make a once-in-a-lifetime visit to the wise master of whom he has heard so much. After an arduous journey, he arrives at the monastery, and waits his turn for a moment with the master. When his turn arrives, he bows in humility and asks the master for a word of enlightenment. The master says simply, "Attention", and turns away to greet the next in line.
>
> The student is stunned. Has he come all this way, through all these hardships, for this? Frustrated, he gets back into the line, and when he finally gets up to the master again, he begs the master. "I don't understand," he says. "Please, just one word more." The master smiles and says, "Of course, I will tell you more. Attention...Attention." He turns to the next in line.
>
> Now the student is truly enraged. After a night of fitful rest, he gets back into the line. When the master sees him approach, he smiles. "I knew you would be back", he says. The student is full of hope; he knows his perseverance will be rewarded. "Yes?" he asks eagerly. The master replies, in a manner that suggests that the matter is completely closed, "Attention...Attention...Attention".[15]

In one of her final essays, Weil suggests that "pure, intuitive attention is the only source of perfectly beautiful art, truly original and brilliant scientific discovery, of philosophy which really aspires to wisdom and of true, practical love of one's neighbor."[16] With this thought in mind, let us now turn to the ways in which we will explore silence in the service of reflective action.

---

[15] "*Ko'ans* are the folk stories of Zen Buddhism, metaphorical narratives that particularize essential nature. Each *ko'an* is a window that shows the whole truth but just from a single vantage. It is limited in perspective. One hundred *ko'ans* give one hundred vantages. When they are enriched with insightful comments and poems, then you have ten thousand vantages. There is no end to this process of enrichment." (Robert Aitken, forward to Book of Serenity, by Thomas Cleary), ix–x. Our thanks to Stephen Billias for sharing this ko'an with us.

[16] Weil, *Gravity and Grace*, 172.

REFERENCES

Aitken, Robert. 1990. Foreword. *Book of Serenity*, Thomas Cleary. Hudson, NY: Lindisfarne Press. ix–x.

Cameron, Sharon. 2003. "The Practice of Attention: Simone Weil's Performance of Impersonality". *Critical Inquiry*, 29:(2). Citation is from "Attention and Will."

Emery, Edward. 1999. Facing 'O': Wilfred Bion, Emmanuel Levinas, and the Face of the Other. Paper presented at "Face to Face With the Real World: Contemporary Applications of Levinas," March 17-19, 1999, Walsh University, Canton, Ohio and at the Ontario Institute for Studies in Education, University of Toronto, in conjunction with the Toronto Institute for Contemporary Psychoanalysis, May 22, 1999. Available at www.psychematters.com/papers/emery1.htm.

Levinas, Emmanuel. *Ethics and Infinity*. 1995. Trans. by Richard Cohen, Pittsburgh: Duquesne University Press.

Otherwise than Being. 1998. Trans. by Alphonso Lingis. Pittsburgh: Duquesne University Press.

Weil, Simone. *Gravity and Grace*. 1952. Trans. A. Wills. New York: Fount Books.

Waiting on God. 1951. Trans. E. Craufurd. New York: Bison Books.

Winnicott, Donald. 1992. "The Observation of Infants in a Set Situation". In *Through Pediatrics to Psychoanalysis: Collected Papers*. New York: Brunner/Mazel.

CHAPTER 2

Working with Silence

Ethics and Silence

What is ethical about considering the role and modes of silence? Paying attention to silence can bridge the gaps created by separateness. Silence liberates the thinker, the decision-maker, and generates the creative innovation of ideas in order to make better decisions.

Enhancing ethics will also enhance and increase effectiveness, efficiency, and equity. Not paying attention to silence, and failing to interpret it correctly, increases the risk of unethical behavior.

As we have seen, silence is always present, but it is often treated as though it exists only at the margins, if anywhere. In this treatise, silence will move from the periphery to center stage. Why? Because we believe that silence can actually ascribe meaning to the context in which any decision will be made. Therefore, we are not interested in "giving voice" to silence for its own sake. Rather, our concern is to observe and analyze the transitions that occur between silence and voice, and to explore fully the interactions that take place between the two.

As we will describe in this chapter, we have selected seven modalities of silence which we feel are key to understanding the interactions that underlie ethical decision-making. This selection is by no means exhaustive; we hope that our work may prove to be a springboard for further exploration. For example, it may well be the case that on occasion people are silent in awe and admiration of those who speak and express their opinion because they believe that they may have the answer to the question at hand.

The advantage of this kind of methodology is that interacting with silence helps us to rediscover the core issue of concern. Silence cannot be defined unconditionally as it is always contextual, as a part of any interaction or communication. The exploration of silence is not the end of any enquiry, but should form a part of it, as it enriches ethical understanding. Methodologically, we believe that asking people to explain their silence(s) is not the most fruitful way to proceed. Instead, we have asked people to reflect on how the various modalities of silence that we have selected find expression in their particular contexts.

We have delineated five steps that we feel are essential to the process of paying attention to, recognizing, and interpreting silence. This is an iterative process: that is, an ongoing dynamic interaction between voice and silence. The five steps are as follows:

1. Pay attention to silence.
2. Experience attention; bring it to consciousness.
3. Analyze the silence through full engagement.
4. Inscribe silence onto one's own thinking.
5. Consciously act on the basis of this reflective process.

Chapter 1 proposed that attention has ethical significance. Now let us turn to the question of paying attention to silence as a foundation for ethical action. One must recognize that silence exists, even if one chooses to ignore it. A problem common to many interactions today is that people often begin a decision-making process with firmly fixed agendas and opinions. In effect, they leave no room for paying attention to silence. This is a fundamentally unethical way of proceeding: it considers only the acting subject. All others (people, ideas) are viewed simply as means towards the ends that the acting subject has in view. From its inception, such an undertaking often results in conflict.

There is some urgency in paying attention to silence. Contemporary society is full of examples of the unintended – and often disastrous – consequences of failing to attend sufficiently well to silence. Take, for example, the current trend towards voter apathy. People are losing – have perhaps already lost – hope and confidence that their voices will be heard. In the 2014 US midterm elections, only 37 percent of registered voters cast a ballot. Unless people are forced to exercise choice, they tend toward silence. Until some change occurs whereby this silence is taken note of, analyzed, and interpreted, this situation will only become worse.

The second step of the process is to experience attention. That is, we ought to recognize where silence is occurring. The cost of ignoring silence is enormous. The debate over universal health care in the USA provides one striking example. A bill was formulated based on a mandate that actually represented only a small minority of the people who would be affected. A tremendous cost was involved in getting the bill passed through the various governmental structures: a cost not only of time and money, but also of suffering on the part of the population at large whom the bill was supposed to serve. Recognizing the lack of representation of the "silent majority" would have improved the efficiency and effectiveness of this initiative, and resulted in a more equitable outcome.

The third step brings us to the stage of analysis, where reflection on the silence of all parties is essential. Such reflection not only recognizes each person at the decision-making table, it also acknowledges and brings into consideration their individual needs and desired outcomes, which may or may not be voiced. At this juncture, an ethical process ought to inquire into the reasons for silence. No one can (or should) be forced to break their silence – but efforts have to be made to understand the silences, and to encourage the participants to assist the group in the interpretation of these.

An example from the world of special needs children may be instructive here. Consider a young person on the autism spectrum who is non-verbal. He wants something to eat. Being non-verbal, he can only look at his caregiver and hope that she understands what he wants. If she does not interpret his silence correctly and move to give him what he wants, the child's frustration may escalate into violent acting out. In this case, the child with autism has no choice but to remain silent. The caregiver must be attuned to the child's patterns of needs and desires in order to interpret the silence correctly and respond accordingly.

The fourth step takes ethics one move further. "Inscribing silence onto one's own actions" is somewhat akin to the management principle that is sometimes known as "the Platinum Rule." The Golden Rule suggests that we treat others as *we* would wish to be treated. In the 1990s, a Platinum Rule began to be discussed: "Treat others the way *they* wish to be treated." The significant distinction between these two practices is that rather than assuming that I know what someone wants, I seek to understand their desires and address them, even though neither the desire nor the resolution may be voiced. Instead of moving immediately into action, I first reflect from my internal silence on a range of possible interpretations of the other's silence: not purely from my own perspective and experience, but as a result of enquiry into the other.

This stance is antithetical to the traditional imperialist, colonialist attitude that has informed so much governmental interaction with indigenous peoples. For example, it is generally assumed by proponents of democracy that its only correct form signifies "one person, one vote." In certain cultures, however, democracy might be more properly conceptualized as "one clan, one vote." Unless one begins with an inquiry into the nature of the democracy that a particular group aspires to, pluralistic versions cannot be accommodated. If some attempt is made to inscribe another's silence onto my own actions, I may begin to understand the reason for such silence. Doing so will result in a much more fruitful discussion.

Conscious action, therefore, is the end result and final step of this iterative process. Awareness by itself is insufficient. What is required for effective change is an informed and mindful transformation through an examination of silence. Ethical decision-making does not begin with a plan of action. Rather, truly ethical decision-making begins in silence. In each of the examples given above, some form of silence was a fundamental precursor to action.

Modalities of Silence

It is often thought that silence is empty. In fact, it is full: of potentiality and of meaning. In addition, silence is not one thing, but rather a plurality. Certainly, decisions must be made in order for change to occur, but if change processes are to be holistic, ethical, and sustainable, one must first seek to understand the modalities of silence.

The many meanings of silence depend to a great extent upon the specific task at hand and on who is involved. For the purposes of this book, we have selected seven key aspects of silence:

- The empty rhetoric
- The insolent silence
- The silence of hopelessness
- The silence of the oppressed
- The silence of fear
- The silence of attentive listening
- The silence which makes space for dialogue

This selection is modeled after a meditation by the twentieth-century Italian Quaker Davide Melodia, describing the eloquence of silence:

> *Some speak... and say nothing.*
> *Some are silent... because they have nothing to say.*
> *Some are silent... to listen.*
> *Some are silent... so as not to tell the truth.*
> *Some are silent... because they are afraid.*
> *Some are silent... because they are proud.*
> *Some are silent... and in their own way eloquent.*[1]

Each of the chapters that follow will explore how these modalities or aspects of silence factor in to decision-making in a number of contexts. (Not all seven will appear in every case.) Our inquiry is focused on four elements of each modality: definition, effect, implications, and the changes that are needed in order to promote transformation.

Empty Rhetoric "Some speak... and say nothing." This modality can be variously interpreted: either by the one who speaks or from the vantage point of the one who hears what is said. One who engages in empty rhetoric by speaking may say, "I speak, but it falls on deaf ears." One who hears nothing, on the other hand, may interpret speech as saying nothing of significance. In both cases, no communication has occurred, and no connectivity is discernible.

This lack of connectivity results in a number of negative consequences, including mistrust, destruction of meaning, and continual erosion of engagement. Interactions of this type are hollow. Although they may seem to connote relationship, in fact no real relationship exists: only one of lip service. It is as though one is following an empty paradigm.

The dominant implication of this modality is a consolidation of preconceived notions, an assumption that each person already knows and understands what the other(s) will say, and that no new conclusions will emerge. A ritualistic, automated reinstatement of one's position may occur: but no real thinking, listening, or presence can ensue. A sort of conceptual circularity begins to take the place of an organic, dynamic framework of meaning. Moral consciousness is set aside, in favor of decisions that are based on misunderstandings of silence. No amount of

---

[1] Davide Melodia, *The Lord of Silence*, no. 19.

noisy posturing about changing fundamental values on any side will yield any favorable outcomes.

When one's viewpoint is immovably fixed, the only speech that occurs is continual restatement of one's position. If each side has an equally fixed position (about the other's silence, for example), the first task must be to unpack and understand the existence of each other's silence. If, on the other hand, one is able to return to the empty space of attention (as described in Chapter 1), one may be liberated from the shackles that fix one's own position. Even if one is unable to move (to change one's position, for example), a turn may be possible: a turn toward the other. This may be where ethics can begin. The turn renders possible and enables discourse which goes beyond dialogue or dialectic, into the realm of infinite, unthought-of possibilities. This is the beginning of the journey towards change.

The Silence of Insolence Another form that silence often takes results from pride. Some may feel that the gap of understanding between people is so great that one does not know where to begin. In addition, pride may entail a lack of willingness to explain one's position. Why should I justify myself in relation to the other, when there is little likelihood of being understood? Bridging the gap may not even be perceived as a desirable outcome. The gulf may seem so wide that the cost to me of reducing it may not seem worth the effort and time required. A cost-benefit comparison may yield the perception that I am giving far more than I am receiving in return.

As with empty rhetoric, one result of perceived disparity is mistrust. In addition, insolence tends to foreclose the possibility of innovative thinking. Pride often closes the door to new ideas. Furthermore, it may lead to profound disregard of, and disrespect for, the other. Insolent silence neither contains nor allows for any system of checks and balances.

Perhaps the most serious implication of this form of silence is the radical assumption of Cartesian dualism: the bipolarity that breaks the world down into binary opposites. The supposition that people can be encapsulated and understood in terms of descriptors that measure difference (black/white; male/female; indigenous/non-indigenous) begins not from a sense of freedom, but from one side of a closed door. The other person is robbed of the opportunity to exist or develop outside of predetermined categories. So am I. There is no winner in this contest. The discussion usually becomes focused on articulating – and worse, tolerating – difference, instead of being with one another in the richness of the silence.

Ethical change will only come about when difference can be understood in terms of the value that may be added, rather than maintaining a protective focus on what may have to be given up. One helpful strategy in this regard may be to return to the moment of attention that precedes action. *Prior* to taking a stance, I am in a liminal position. If I have not yet committed to any particular point of view, and conscious attempt to maintain a suspension of judgment. Perhaps from that standpoint, I can become aware not only of my difference from the other, but also my responsibility for the other.

The Silence of Hopelessness "Some are silent…because they have nothing to say." Silence may arise when someone has expressed himself over and over again, and has now lost all hope that his voice will be heard or attended to. This is the silence of despair, which denotes disempowerment and disenfranchisement. It may be misunderstood as laziness, indifference, or an unwillingness to become part of the system. Therefore the silenced people's very existence is problematized: rather than being seen as acting subjects, they become objects to be investigated or managed.

Those who are silent may well have something to say: a deep conviction that they are not perceived to be part of the system. They have a crisis of belonging. In this group may be found those who can't even make it to the first rung of the developmental ladder, economically or politically. They try to belong, but their voice is indistinct, if acknowledged at all. How can their voice come to be heard in the decision-making process?

Another effect of hopeless silence is the emergence of a black-market mentality. Feeling invisible within the mainstream, people may desire to create an alternative system, where they *can* be represented fully, where their voices *can* be heard. The results of this mentality include drug addiction, prostitution and the like. Hopelessness may take many forms, from escapism (by various methods) to extremism.

Several implications follow this modality of silence. Perhaps the most serious is the loss of a sense of agency. This has a twofold effect. First, any policy that is enacted tends to lack effectiveness because that policy bypasses lived reality. Yet those without agency are blamed for the policy's failure. Thus the poor are blamed for being poor in the first place, and for staying poor.

The second effect of loss of agency is that the hopeless may no longer have a sense of self-worth. This cycle becomes a self-fulfilling prophecy: hopeless behavior perpetuates a lack of motivation on the part of those who have repeatedly but fruitlessly voiced distress. The failure of trickle-down economics is a testament to this form of silence. Institutions may emerge to redress the imbalance, but if they are not attuned to this form of silence, they follow the same path to failure.

Along with the lack of self-worth comes a questioning of traditional roles and values. The crisis of belonging becomes a crisis of identity. If I can no longer fulfill the role of father/provider, for example, how can I understand who I am? It is easy to see how lack of self-worth devolves into instability in families and marriages.

One further implication of hopelessness should be noted here: the fear of being forgotten. If I feel that I am invisible and unheard, my only identity may be that of one who is "lost," a person with no social standing. In this case, I may feel that the only role available for me to play in society is a role outside the framework of the mainstream, including the law. Offering incentives to hopeless people is ineffective; it produces only short-term and superficial changes in behavior.

True change can be effected by helping people to re-find a voice within the mainstream. One important initiative here has to be an increased emphasis on mental health. Before focusing on economic well-being, much more attention should be paid to emotional well-being. A healthy sense of self-worth provides the foundation for empowerment, and for taking responsibility for one's own actions and voice. Reinstituting agency will help bring people back into the decision-making arena.

The Silence of the Oppressed "Some are silent... so as not to tell the truth." This form of silence includes both subjective speaking and subjective listening. The oppressed say whatever they think the other wants to hear. The motivation for this type of silence arises from two factors: the presence of different value systems, and the complexity of decision-making processes. Thus, the motivation to suppress information may not be malicious, though it may appear to be so. It may seem that I am hiding information from you, and you may question my agenda in so doing. Your reaction may be one of resistance and mistrust. What are you hiding from me, and why? Don't I have the right to the same information as you have in order to have the same level of power as you? Allow me to choose what I want to take and to discard. Give me the power and authority of self-determination.

An example from Aboriginal tradition is replicated in all Indigenous contexts. Some Indigenous societies in Australia have a "three-door policy" when it comes to engaging in consultation with the mainstream. Each house has three doors. The first door is open to everyone, and provides only superficial knowledge of a situation. The second door is for those who are culturally attuned, and participate in a relationship of mutual trust. The third door, to the innermost core of the reality of the situation, is open to only a select few. One must consider carefully the consequences of entering through the third door. Doing so entails a form of transformation into someone else's worldview. It also entails the responsibilities accompanying that worldview, which may or may not be palatable.

Those who are silent because of oppression may also be prompted to this silence because of the sheer complexity of decision-making processes. At the best of times, decision-making involving multiple agents is tricky. However, the complexity is multiplied when dealing with a fractured or broken other. My truth may be complex, and I may not trust that you will understand it. Both sides suffer from this same anxiety regarding misinterpretation of the complexity of their perceived truth. From this position, the ensuing conversation can only involve omission of certain aspects of "truth." This leads to misunderstanding of the reasons why people do not share information with others. The other is "broken" because I do not see her in her entirety as a person; I only see elements of her.

This modality of silence can have severe repercussions. The dominant party may seek to superimpose a value system of oppression onto the other. Such a move will inevitably create resistance. Then, partners in the interaction may try to impose their agenda on the process, resulting in stalemate. Everyone then becomes entrenched: not only with regard to position, but also with respect to power. The grim silence of an impasse is the all-too-frequent result.

In order to bring about change, a return to the valuing of pluralistic views is required. First, each person's truth must be heard, acknowledged, and respected. Returning for a moment to the fivefold process outlined earlier, change will only come once I have inscribed the other's silence onto my own thinking. Doing so will enable me to reframe my approach to the situation and may allow me to locate a point of intersection with the other. Rather than either side seeking to appropriate the methodology of the other, a new methodology should be created which gives equal power and equal voice to all concerned. The procedures and protocols which flow from this new methodology need not be the same for all parties.

Commonality does not mean giving up one's own framework; rather, new frameworks may be added.

The Silence of Fear "Some are silent... because they are afraid." Fear can be a powerful and varied stimulus for silence. Misinterpretation of my truth may be the least consequential. Deeper than that lies the fear of vulnerability or even of shame: if I break my silence and reveal my truth to you, what will you do with this knowledge about me? Even if it is heard and understood, will it be used against me in some way?

The other may also experience a fear resulting from silence. Am I, the oppressed, being silent because I am withholding something from you? Am I, in collusion with others, silently plotting against you? The oppressor fears an uprising. He may also be silent in order not to give too much away.

The effects of fear may cover a wide range: from concern regarding social backlash, to anxiety over the possible repercussions to one's actions, to what the United Nations has constituted as the criterion for being awarded refugee status: "a well-founded fear of persecution." (It is important to reiterate here that this book is focused on looking at the phenomenon of silence as a part of decision-making processes, not on those who have been silenced.) I may keep silent in order not to upset someone, or in order to forward my agenda, or simply in the hopes of being retained within the process. In more severe cases, I may choose to keep silent simply in order to survive, whether this is in the context of an abusive relationship, a hostile work environment, or ethnic cleansing.

The implications of this form of silence can be equally powerful. Not voicing one's needs (out of a fear of social disapprobation) may lead to marginalization by agencies (a further disenfranchisement of voice). Choosing silence out of fear may provoke increased aggression from others. Intimidating behavior may be used as a reinforcement of authority, ultimately resulting in the creation of a culture of fear. In the most extreme circumstances, this modality of silence leads to utter depersonalization.[2]

---

[2] Giorgio Agamben provides an example of such depersonalization with his description of the *Muselmann* who could sometimes be found in concentration camps during the Holocaust. The term originally meant "Muslim," but came to denote those people who had utterly given up hope, and were so weak and abject that they were no longer seen as subjects even by fellow inmates. See Agamben, *Remnants of Auschwitz*, ch. 2.

The onus of responsibility to address the fear is on all sides. On the one side, the mainstream must put systems in place to foster the courage and strength of those who are silent out of fear, so that all can freely express their opinions without thinking about negative ramifications. How can mutual trust be enhanced? One way is to encourage the development of programs that empower people to realize their full potential. Rather than seeing themselves as policymakers, it would be more helpful for governments to see themselves as facilitators of environments of empowerment. On the other side, people who are silent out of fear need to respond by becoming directly involved in the process of decision-making, and working toward an atmosphere of mutual respect.

The Silence of Attentive Listening "Some are silent... to listen." This kind of silence is rooted in attention, as discussed in Chapter 1. However, the silence of attentive listening has a number of elements. Its aim is to achieve mutual understanding. Concentration is central to this form of silence: it requires a calm focused presence to both what is being said and what is not being said. Such silence must be accomplished mindfully: that is, without any preconceived framework, bias or interpretations. In essence, this type of silence is contemplative: it is only possible when the individuals are centered and approach the process with no agenda of their own.

The effects of this modality are to enable constructive engagement and to empower all participants equitably. Attentive listening has a mediative quality. It seeks to create common ground amongst all participants. Constructive dialogue can then begin: a free flow of ideas and suggestions for action. If managed properly, this form of silence possesses much potential for generating positive effects.

The silence of attentive listening results in the development of policies that will tend to be more effective, efficient, equitable, and ethical. As we will see in the case studies that follow, an array of mediation strategies are needed to bridge existing gaps (which will depend, to some extent, on context). In some cases, advocacy will be required: in others, the emphasis will be on reconciliation, on arbitration, on remediation or some other approach.

The task of transformation in this modality centers on the issue of complexity. Attentive silence begins by building recognition of, and tolerance for, multilayered conceptualizations. Once one is on the road to understanding complexity, strategies for its management can be suggested. As we listen to each other's silence, we begin to make connections between our different knowledge bases. Continued listening allows us to transcend our own knowledge boundaries, and inscribe elements of others' knowledge into ours. Through this process, hope is created, which enables one to look toward and plan for the future.

The Silence Which Makes Space for Dialogue   "Some are silent... and in their own way eloquent." Every voice or set of voices has a complementary set of silences: communication, and indeed all human interaction, comes into being within a plurality of silence. Silence and sound coexist and interact at the core of every decision process. Every decision is accompanied by some kind of silence. That silence has unintended corollaries. For example, a great deal of contextual information is transmitted through the silence. The silence makes mutual presencing possible Thus, we can reach towards understanding amongst all participants. Understood in its entirety, this modality of silence makes room for otherness. It constitutes movement towards wholeness and inclusion. It helps us to experience each other more fully and to create new knowledge bases, in which knowledge is critically incorporated from all sides. This modality of silence is not based on a deficit approach, but rather on an attitude of empathy, which allows accommodation of the other, and of the other's silence. This modality is fluid, dynamic, and interactive. It enables discourse rather than merely descriptive analysis.

This modality provides a space for dialogue. In this setting, a new category can be envisaged: an active, silent other who is attentively present to the process; neutral, and oriented toward the future. This "other" can think and plan proactively rather than merely reactively. One further effect of this modality will be that interdisciplinarity will be more widely embraced as a methodology – in both the weak and the strong senses indicated in Chapter 1.

As this occurs, new schools of thought will emerge. First, a new, more positive dualism will appear, in contradistinction to the traditional paradigm. Then, new branches of understanding will arise, leading to a multiplicity of thought.

It will be vital to protect these new ways of thinking from being hijacked by the mainstream. The tendency is for new ideas to be initially rejected by the mainstream, then marginalized. When the strategy of pushing unwelcome intruders to the periphery proves ineffective, these ideas are then appropriated and co-opted by the mainstream, in an attempt to reinscribe the new as a recurrence of the familiar. Instead, as tension builds between the mainstream and new ways of thinking, creative silence will work on maintaining the space of freedom in which this process can continue to replenish itself.

In fact, the change brought about by considering this modality calls for a paradigm shift. This is an evolutionary, rather than a revolutionary progression. History is thus no longer conceived of as definitive or determined. Rather, the past is freed by silence to become a means of awareness. This change in thinking invites us to recognize silence as a distinct and unique method with its own underlying theory, epistemology, and pedagogy.

The modalities of silence which we have discussed in this chapter have been represented by describing how knowledge and understanding are applied, normalized, and created through recognition, articulation, and action. Combining reflection on the past with observation of conditions and interactions in the present, these modalities facilitate a new vision of the future. Silence can be described in epistemological terms as prescriptive, descriptive, or evolutionary. Adopting a systems approach, we can conceptualize silence as static, mechanistic, dialectical, and conflict-producing, or we can as dynamic, fluid, interdependent, and relationship-building. In discursive terms, it could be normative, interpretive, dialogical, critical, and/or interdisciplinary in nature. Depending on the type of inquiry, it can be described as technical, practical, emancipatory, and/or as representing vested interests. Finally, in terms of co-ordination, silence can be used as a textured tool that can be applied for mutual engagement and/or disengagement. It can also be used as a point of departure from which accommodation can begin, the neutrality of existing tools can be established, and new tools can be created.

Silence is ubiquitous and complex, yet no theory exists to encapsulate or ground its examination. Thus, following Yin's recommendation, we will continue our exploration into creative silence by adopting a case analysis methodology.

Methodology

Case Selection Criteria No single theory has as yet been expounded to articulate a comprehensive definition of silence. Neither has there been, to our knowledge, any interdisciplinary inquiry into this topic. In order to begin to understand the diverse uses of silence, in the chapters that follow, we will present findings from a variety of contemporary settings. Our aim is to look at how and why people pay attention to silence, and to develop a framework for understanding that is thoroughly rooted in reality. The cases that we have selected give voice to practitioners in different disciplines, contexts, and geographic regions.

The first criterion for case selection is contextual. Each case is practitioner-oriented, and is explored from within the particularities of its context. Practitioners from a multiplicity of fields are involved: not simply from the health care sector, but from education, environmentalism, economics, and so on.

The next criterion is continuity. This means that the data from the cases is collected in real time. The study is unfolding continuously, even as we examine it. We could have selected from any number of real-world scenarios because a crucial determinant for us was the inclusion of illustrations from around the globe. We had no choice but to limit our selection in order to keep the project manageable.

The third criterion measures change. It entails a modification of the lens through which practitioners view both themselves and their work. In each case, the findings do not consist merely of records of participant observation. Rather, the thrust of our inquiry is on the reflections of practitioners as to how each modality of silence is recognized, interpreted, and managed within the context of their sphere of influence.

More specifically, a fourth criterion examines the nature of cooperation. The emphasis in each case is on analysis of how practitioners and participants move between the spaces of the various modalities. We were led to this emphasis by political philosopher William Desmond's study of communities, in which he suggests that

> [t]he self and the other are together in the between; but the self and the other are themselves modes of togetherness; they duplicate modes of togetherness; neither constitutes the between from out of itself; this is an impossibility. The community of the between is neither in here nor out there, for it is in here and out there, it is everywhere and nowhere. The self and the other are in the field of communication, and are themselves fields of communication.[3]

---

[3] William Desmond, *Being and the Between: Political Theory in the American Academy*, 445.

The final criterion aims at consistency and is measured over time. Ultimately, for our work to be effective and meaningful, practitioners had to have and take the time to react to our reflection on their findings.

Analysis Methodology We elected to draw upon the findings in our cases by utilizing a six-stage method. In the first stage, practitioners were briefed about the modalities that we have identified. We asked the practitioners to validate the existence of the modalities we specified, and to modify the categories according to the actual situations in which they (the practitioners) were involved. Thus, in some cases, new modalities had to be considered. In others, it became evident that not all of the modalities we had anticipated were present. In addition, some modalities were more salient in certain contexts than in others. Thus, practitioners were asked to identify which modalities were present, and then to assign weights to each.

The second stage was to ask practitioners how they managed these modalities of silence as they appeared. We asked them to provide a narrative description of the management of each modality. In this way we hoped to reduce the subjective bias of observation. At the same time, however, we wanted to gather more than formulaic facts and figures.

We then asked practitioners to reflect on the steps that they used of our fivefold process of paying attention to silence. Were all five steps used – and useful? Did they find that the steps presented themselves in the order which we had specified? This research process is dialogical in nature. The analysis is directed toward discovery of similarities. Therefore, the data that we were collecting should be under the paradigm of structural variation, where the preliminary standpoint may shift in the course of the investigation. This activity required that the practitioner be open to the possibility that new concepts may emerge.

Having received the narrative data from our partners in the field, the next phase of the inquiry was for us to analyze the findings both within the case itself as well as across cases. The first step of this phase was to provide a comprehensive contextualization of both the practitioner and his/her setting. This aspect of the work was both biographic and bibliographic. We needed to explore who the practitioners were, in terms of theoretical backgrounds, assumptions, and motivations. We also needed to locate them in the context of their disciplinary orientation. Having examined each case individually in this manner, a cross-case pattern analysis was essential to bring coherence to our understanding of the modalities of silence.

At this point, it was significant that practitioners were given an opportunity to validate and comment upon our results. In order to keep the process of inquiry "live," it was not sufficient for us merely to attach theoretical constructs to the data provided. From start to finish, this was an interactive process and a truly interdisciplinary framework.

The final step of the project was to return to our original ideas about silence, and critically evaluate the modalities of silence we had identified, reformulating them if and as necessary. Only in this way could we hope to close the hermeneutic loop.

Interdisciplinary Methodology   As we noted at the outset, we feel that an interdisciplinary approach is most helpful in understanding the modalities of silence. In the course of this project, therefore, we have followed an interdisciplinary structure and method throughout.

Most of the work that has been carried out on decision-making – whether in applied economics or in applied philosophy – has not done more than to touch upon the question of ethical modes of silence. The confines of a single discipline fail to do adequate justice to unraveling the significance and the complexity of this powerful aspect of communication.

Often, silence is merely used as a metaphor in the decision-making process. But what is a metaphor? George Kalamaras points out that according to Aristotle, a metaphor is above all else, that which "gives clearness, charm, and distinction to the style...which echoes Plato's mistrust of that which is ambiguous."[4] It is the very process of reaching towards an ideal that provides the misrepresentation of reality in the quest for understanding. Theory prefers to stay in the realm of pure abstraction. But reality – lived practice – especially with regard to ethics, is both "dirty" and complicated. Our original intention was to understand how an exploration of creative silence could be transformative to social processes. Kalamaras elaborates:

> In this discussion on metaphor, we see a similarity between silence and language. Such a transformative quality is what gives metaphor, like the practice of silence, its generative capacity to evoke paradoxical perceptions that the realm of conceptual understanding alone cannot accomplish. Most significantly, metaphor...has the power to conjure – and not merely

---

[4] George Kalamaras, *Reclaiming the Tacit Dimension: Symbolic form in the Rhetoric of silence,* 130.

represent – an awareness of simultaneity and psychic fluidity, a realm where subject and object unite.[5]

Furthermore, silence is continuously evolving. Like language, it exists as a process of continual interpretation. Fuller understanding comes through abandoning – or at least shifting beyond – disciplinary bias and theoretical rhetoric. Each discipline binds its proponents into a modality of interpretation and locks others out of the conversation through the use of discipline-specific jargon. In writing this book, for instance, we experienced moments in which words or phrases were used by one of us which had virtually no meaning for the other: from the economist, words like "aggregation" and "up-skilling"; from the philosopher, terms like "deontological" and "apophatic." The use of such terms by one of us always resulted in reducing the other to an amused silence. This is one more reason why we perceive a need for greater interdisciplinarity, especially in the service of ethics.

It has been instructive for us to bear in mind that, in an interdisciplinary exchange of ideas, it is the subject matter, rather than the discipline, which directs the inquiry. If two disciplines are working together, it is not a question of each contributing 50 percent. The exchange cannot be quantified into a transactional trade-off between disciplines. In fact, to give voice to the other means to recognize that the other has more to contribute to your discipline than you could imagine. It is equally important, however, to recognize that in working across disciplines, no attempt is being made to create a new discipline. No new jargon is created and no search for pedagogy is entered into.

We outlined in Chapter 1 a distinction between strong and weak interdisciplinarity. This distinction is the basis of our methodology, as illustrated in the organization of the chapters and sections of this book.

The methodology begins with examples of weak interdisciplinarity: that is, an approach that blends at least two academic disciplines. Thus, Chapter 1 is a conversation between philosophy, psychoanalytic theory, and economics. Chapter 2 has continued in this same vein, in a preliminary and primarily theoretical examination of various modalities of silence, and then demonstrating how one might build an interdisciplinary framework of inquiry. In writing these chapters, we began to imagine how

---

[5] Ibid., 79.

interdisciplinary research as a whole could fruitfully use the fivefold method that we use in that chapter to explore silence. We began to envision how this method could be used to explore any number of concepts and constructs.

Chapters 3–10, the case analysis chapters, move into the realm of strong interdisciplinarity, by incorporating the voices and reflections of practitioners alongside, and in conversation with, academic thought. These chapters draw upon examples of individuals in the ordinary course of their lives and practice as they interpret silence.

The final chapter looks to the future. Here we consider what the use of an interdisciplinary method has taught us. How has it enriched our thinking about silence and how it might be managed? In the course of translating our theoretical constructs, how have they been affected? How does critical reasoning begin, in an interdisciplinary context? Finally, how can we locate opportunities in which this interdisciplinary methodology might be used? What is the process by which it can begin?

The challenge of using such a methodology is that the analysis does not end. In bringing this undertaking to a temporal closure, we have applied the "stopping criterion" or convergence criterion used by computer programmers. If further iterations and interactions do not make a substantial contribution to greater (future) understanding, and if participants – who are the real practitioners – do not benefit from contributing to further interactions, the methodology has served its purpose, and can be considered both successful and valid.

It is our hope that the "culture of practice" of thinking about, using, and managing silence becomes a normative aspect of scholarship, both within and across disciplinary boundaries.

REFERENCES

Agamben, Giorgio. 1999. *Remnants of Auschwitz: The Witness and the Archive.* New York: Zone Books.
Desmond, William. 1995. *Being and the Between: Political Theory in the American Academy.* New York: SUNY Press.
Kalamaras, George. 1994. *Reclaiming the Tacit Dimension: Symbolic Form in the Rhetoric of Silence.* New York: SUNY Press.
Melodia, Davide. Nd. *The Lord of Silence.* Available online at: http://www.quaker.org/melodia/silence.

CHAPTER 3

Whose Silence? Hearing Echoes of Disembodied Trauma (Argentina)

> **Respondent Background**
> **Dr. Cristina Santos**
> Dr. Cristina Santos is an Associate Professor of Hispanic and Latin American Studies at Brock University in St. Catharine's, Ontario. Her approach and training is interdisciplinary: she is also involved in teaching in the undergraduate Women's and Gender Studies program and interdisciplinary graduate programs in Comparative Literature and Arts, and PhD in Interdisciplinary Humanities. Some of her current research looks at the "transnational practice of mothering in Latina diasporic communities in Canada and the United States." She is also concerned with the construction of notions of political and social deviance and the intersection of these constructions with personal narrative, identity and trauma.
> Cristina has personal experience of these matters. She was born in Angola in 1972. Her mother was born in Angola, and her father had moved there from Portugal as a teenager. Her first memories are of fleeing the country during the revolution in 1975. She recalls being thrust down in a moving car, experiencing only "darkness and the pop, pop, pop of machine guns." The family was motivated to leave Angola once Portugal had granted Angola its independence and all Portuguese colonists were expected to leave. They were assisted by

© The Author(s) 2017
N. Billias, S. Vemuri, *The Ethics of Silence*,
DOI 10.1007/978-3-319-50382-0_3

South African soldiers to flee Angola to a Red Cross refugee camp in South Africa. After some time in the camp, they were able to get to Portugal. They might have remained there (since Angola had been a Portuguese colony), but her brother was 16, so – since military inscription was still mandatory – her family feared that he might be conscripted to return to Angola to fight. The family immigrated to Canada and relocated to Oshawa.

In Canada, they followed the traditional refugee trajectory of starting from nothing and engaging in education in the interest of upward social mobility. (Sadly, her brother died of a heart attack at the age of 30.) Cristina moved swiftly and smoothly through higher education, gaining an undergraduate degree in English and Spanish Literature, and completing her doctorate in Latin American studies in 2001.

Historical and Cultural Context Argentina's "Dirty War" had its origins in the military coup of 1955 which ousted progressive Marxist leader Juan Peron into exile after three terms as President. Peron had made serious attempts to reform the Argentinian economy with a blend of capitalist and socialist ideals known as "Justialismo." After his removal from office, a repressive and reactionary government reinstated the traditional oligarchy, establishing a brutal, quasi-military totalitarian regime under the guise of "democracy."

During the 18 years of Peron's exile, several attempts were made by insurgent groups to overthrow the government, using both rural and urban guerrilla tactics. When Peron returned to power in 1973, he was able to bring together a number of these groups. He died in 1974. His widow, Isabel Peron, ruled for a very brief period, but her base was unstable, and a military junta gained power in 1975.

The efforts of the military government to solidify power and remove any opposition were carried out from 1976 to 1983. During this time, anyone suspected of dissident or subversive behavior was considered a "social deviant" and subject to kidnap, arrest, detention and interrogation. These people – guilty or innocent – were taken to secret detention centers, where they were often tortured or killed. Many were taken by aircraft to just outside the city limits of Buenos Aires and pushed from the plane into the sea, so that their bodies could not be recovered or identified. Pregnant women were often kept in detention until their babies were born, at which point some of the children were allowed to stay with their mothers, while some were sent to live with family members; many other children were "adopted" by families loyal to the military government. Children whose parents "disappeared" were similarly "adopted."

The Dirty War was conducted openly for seven years in the midst of one of the largest cities in Latin America. A deep complicity of silence, rooted in fear, allowed this practice to continue until a civilian government was finally reinstituted in 1983.

The silence did not end with the war, however. Today, 40 years later, people in Argentina are still reluctant to speak about the Dirty War and those who "disappeared," for many reasons. Some still fear reprisals or the reopening of old wounds. The children who were "adopted" may be loath to discover that the parents who raised them were somehow complicit in the brutality of the Dirty War.

Case Analysis Throughout her career, Cristina's research has focused on the silence of women, specifically the silence of Latin American women. She feels that "culture has largely silenced women's experience," that women have traditionally not spoken out for fear of censorship or anxiety about being considered "deviant." For Cristina, her work on testimony is about breaking women's silence. She stated that she has become a "more politicized silence practitioner" over the past ten years as a result of two experiences that she regards as "life-changing."

The first of these experiences took place in 2010. She had met her colleague Adriana Spahr in 1996. Prof. Spahr is an Associate Professor of Latin American Studies at MacEwan University in Edmonton, Canada. The two women met as graduate students at the University of Toronto and had developed a close friendship over the years, supporting one another through illnesses and infertility issues, births and deaths.

Yet it was not until they had known one another for nearly *ten years* that Prof. Spahr revealed that she had spent seven and a half years as a political prisoner in Argentina.

> The topic had come up occasionally but it never came out. I knew theoretically what had occurred to her. But to hear the story of my very close friend... the fact that it took her close to ten years to reveal that story shows a really weighty past. She trusted me, but still could not speak about it – the trauma had held her back for so long. We cried, we hugged. In that moment, there were no words.

The second life-changing moment occurred in 2015, when she took some students from Canada to Argentina to view the historical sites from the Dirty War which are being dedicated to memorialization. The course was called "Em/bodying Trauma" and was for 4th year Women's Studies and Gender Studies students and a doctoral student pursuing research in memorialization and trauma studies. The course entailed two weeks of intensive reading at Brock University and then two weeks of site visits and lectures in Buenos Aires. The curriculum was focused on trauma, recovery, working through silence, and what it means to listen.

Cristina, with the participation of Prof. Spahr, took the students on three site visits in Buenos Aires. The first was to the Olimpo Garage, a former bus depot, which had been used during the Dirty War as a clandestine detention center. The garage is located in a very quiet residential area of the city, across the street from a primary school which had remained in use throughout this period. In their preparatory material, students had read several contemporary reports in which people had said "We never heard anything – it couldn't have been there" when questioned about the use of the space as a detention center. The silence of denial had been quite loud in the reports.

As the group toured silently around the site, nothing remarkable occurred. Then they came to a room in which scrapbooks from the families had been assembled, each family trying to reconstitute their "disappeared" relative. At this point, Prof. Spahr had to leave; she found the silence overwhelming. It brought back too vividly memories of her years as a political prisoner.

The authorities had tried to cover up the history of the cells by asphalting over the cell walls. Each cell was just long enough to lie down in, with a width of 2½ feet. Viewing the cells in silence, the group took in the physical and spiritual corporeality of the prisoners' experience. At one point, they walked around the perimeter of the building – at which time Cristina spoke very quietly to Prof. Spahr, who was standing in front of the school opposite the garage. She could be heard quite clearly. How was it, then, that for six years no one heard the screams of prisoners being interrogated?

The second site the group visited was the Park of Memory, close to the River Plate which runs through Buenos Aires to the ocean. In the park, a large memorial wall consisting of three distinct walls has been erected in the shape of a scar. The wall bears a name plate for each one of the 30,000 disappeared and/or murdered men, women (including pregnant women) and children. The youngest child who has been identified was 12 years old.

The location of the park by the side of the river is very significant. When the army began the "death flights," they did not fly out very far towards the ocean. However, as time went on, this method had to be modified; if they did not fly out far enough, the tides would bring the bodies back up the river towards the city, providing a silent witness to the violence. Thus, over time, the planes began to fly out further and further.

As of 2015, eight sculptures have been completed in the park, out of an eventual seventeen. From wherever one stands, one is always conscious of the river in the background. The park and the monuments are peaceful, designed for contemplation; the only noise is a waterfall running down the back of one of the walls. The wall itself represents a physical rupture of silence placed between the past and the present.

Cristina records that the visit to the Park of Memory was the most difficult for the students. They couldn't take the magnitude of the number of victims, and the juxtaposition of the peacefulness of the park with the wall with the names. The students became emotional, unable to control their affective response, and started crying. They had to stop thinking about what they had witnessed, and for about half an hour went to different parts of the park "to allow the silence to become less loud."

The final visit was to one of the worst sites of the Dirty War: to the military academy that had been used as a concentration camp. After touring the buildings and grounds from the outside, the final stop of the guided tour was what had been the officers' mess hall, which has been converted into a museum.

The site still looks like a residential military academy, with residences reached via a security gate with checkpoint. When prisoners were brought in, they were always hooded and usually stuffed in the bottom of a car. At that time, a senior student was generally stationed at the checkpoint. The basement level of the museum recreates the intake process that prisoners would undergo: interrogation, fingerprinting, and being stripped of their clothing. Each morning, the death flight list would be compiled in the main meeting room: – the officers' mess hall. The next level consisted of rooms for officers. The prisoners' cubicles were in the attic. In one, a single chair represents a prisoner being held in isolation. In another, several chairs represent shared detention. The sound of old-fashioned typewriters fills the silence; prisoners were often put to work doing research on "subversives." The main hall is a huge whitewashed room.

Numerous empty picture frames line the walls, into which at least twenty LCD projectors project display pictures of the disappeared, the officers, of everything that was done and suffered there, both in still photos and television clips. When one enters the room, there are only pictures and no sound. Then the sound starts to build: the sounds of military equipment and personnel, of those imprisoned, tortured, and disappeared.

At this point, Cristina "couldn't take it, it was all too much." She started to cry and found that she could not catch her breath. She felt claustrophobic. She says,

> I went into silence at that point. I experienced a feeling of being totally powerless and overwhelmed...Went out and cried. "How can I ever do something that can make a difference?" The rest of the day [was an] internalized moment of self-reflection. I didn't want to talk about it." I am a very spiritual person, on that level, it overwhelmed me. Spiritually, rationally, physically. It was only a few days later that I was able to begin to process it.

This case revealed a fascinating new set of insights about silence. From the outset, Cristina's professional experiences were interwoven on several levels with her personal history and with the history of those whom she was studying. As the interview continued, the dynamic nature of silence became ever more clear and significant. Ultimately, the silences she encountered in her research subjects and in her own methodology, only became intelligible as the product of a multi-faceted process, which was mediated to her by the silence of her friends, colleagues, and students.

When she was introduced to the fivefold process of attending to silence which we had delineated, Cristina stated that her Argentina trip was an embodiment of that process. The interview validated two key points: first, that the five aspects of the process were all integral to the development of a deep understanding of silence that could move someone from discovery to action, and second, that the process is not linear but dynamic. Cristina noted the presence of each of the steps, but she did not experience them as occurring sequentially. Rather, they were intricately interwoven into her experience.

As the product of a process, it is helpful if silence undergoes a detailed and reflective analysis. The silence surrounding those whom the Argentinian government removed from public life was shared – from a variety of perspectives – by the victims themselves, their families and loved ones, the perpetrators, and the witnesses. The junta could not have carried out these brutal activities without knowing that they could rely on the silent collusion of the population at large, who were afraid for their own lives, and on the collaboration of the military families and systems who facilitated these actions. Not only was the government actively silencing all who did not support them, they were also energetically inculcating a long-lasting culture of silence which continues to the present day. Silence begat silence. People were, and continue to be, reluctant to break their chosen silence; they do not want to reopen old wounds, challenge old assumptions, and so on. Some people choose to be silent because the reconstruction of memory is too painful, or perhaps they need closure to begin a healing process. Arguably, such healing cannot begin until a locus for reflection has been established, and the precondition for doing so is the acknowledgment and recognition of the original reason for the silence. Once you begin to breed silence, a continual cycle develops, either implicitly or explicitly, as we shall see.

Our research interest is not historical, but ethical. Thus, our focus is not so much in exploring the act of *being* silenced, but rather the *effects* of that act: the quality and nature of the silence itself. How can this silence be understood? And, once understood, how can it be explored and managed, to create a more ethical future?

What does it mean, in this case, to begin by paying attention to silence? As this case disclosed, people choose to be silent for many reasons, including fear of reprisal, a desire to forget trauma, a coping strategy, and out of a lack of awareness of the other. If we hope to suggest strategies for transforming society through a deeper appreciation of silence, we will need to first carry out two tasks. A more thorough analysis will bring the many layers of silence to consciousness. This analysis will then help us to look at ways in which a new equilibrium might be achieved.

The silence that Cristina recounted was deeply context-specific, constructed by an excess or surfeit of historical and political influences. As long as people are encased within the culture of their silence, how can they move towards healing? In order for the meaning of silence to come to consciousness, an environment must be created which can facilitate movement through and out of the silence – a progression that is also a transgression, and which can lead to transformation.

Cristina's own experience illustrates this possibility. As she says in her journal of May 14, 2015, "[At the park] we saw...a reclaiming of death, of memory, of pain to a site of remembrance – not forgetting." The aim of the reflective analysis of silence is to create an environment in which people can begin to see, acknowledge and come to terms with their own relationship to silence, so that they can think about how to transcend their contextual boundaries.

> There was an eeriness about the place – even though the sun shone brightly, birds were chirping loudly – forgotten voices? Silenced voices that even nature is acknowledging and giving voice to? Meanwhile, children on the other side of the bricked-up windows and concrete walls played and giggled on their way to school. It was an ironic play on the senses and on my psyche. I felt immersed in a cloud...inexplicable...a rather recent past, swirling back to speak of the souls lost, the souls who fought – all surviving! "¡¡*Presente!!*"[1]

Cristina felt that she could hear the voices of the disappeared saying, in the silence, "We are here: now and forever!" The silence created at the site enabled her to feel their reclaimed presence.

> My most visceral reaction came from the torture room, which doubled as the carpenter's workroom, repairing furniture sacked from the kidnappings...it entered through my pores...right to my very core...a tightening of my stomach. Not pity. But re-vindication. Re-vindication of giving voice to the silence – through spreading their stories – to educating the next generations.

Her experience of being engulfed by the silence she encountered in Argentina changed her profoundly. Paradoxically, the act of sharing the experience with her students helped her to break through the labyrinth of silences that she had traversed all her life. This entailed a profound change of her own relationship to silence.

Cristina' early experiences had led her to choose a silence of conscious denial. Growing up, she had always tried to remain deliberately unaware of the political:

> [It was] my own conscious choice to silence that part [of life], because growing up I was inundated at the dinner table with all the stories of politics of why we left Angola...I appreciated the stories because they are a part of

---

[1] Cristina Santos, Personal Journal, May 14, 2015. "¡Presente!" is what one says in answer to a roll call: "Here!"

me, but I didn't want the politics. I would not read the paper, switched off news about politics. [This was an] intentional rejection: "I don't want to hear it!"

When she went to Argentina, the silence she encountered surrounding political violence prompted a shift *away* from silence, back to conscious reflection on and expression around violence which she had repressed as a child. Now she felt impelled to speak, to re-voice the stories that she had heard. She recognized within herself a compulsion to examine the bodily, psychosocial influences of trauma. Cristina realized that she was seeking to answer some of her own questions through her research.

> Ironically, halfway through the semester, my father died unexpectedly. He died just before reading week, which was our midterm break. I came back, and standing in front of this same group, I reflected on my own experience of mourning and grieving. I thought about how one could speak about breaking down the culture of silence in Argentina, how it affects the culture of silence when there is no body to mourn.

Although silence is context-specific, the process of understanding is transferable. The silences she encountered in Argentina enabled Cristina to reach through the silence she had constructed around her own early experiences. Visiting the memorial sites, Cristina and her students experienced both the power and the powerlessness of silence. For Cristina, her father's death was the final catalyst through which paying attention to silence could be brought to consciousness, enabling her to inscribe silence more fully into her thought processes. She could then become the medium through which the process could be transmitted to her students.

Cristina recounts that she began to teach very differently after her experiences of silence in Buenos Aires. She became more politicized, both in and out of the classroom. She became involved (and involved students) with NGOs serving the large population of immigrants, refugees and migrant workers in the local community, people who had been, up to that time, largely invisible to the majority of the local community. Having encountered real people, rather than abstractions, they were able to understand what Cristina was teaching in a completely new way. Now the knowledge came home to them: they were no longer motivated by "what would be on the test." Now they had encountered real people to whom such things had happened. Thus, the next time she taught her "Testimony" course, she noticed a substantive shift; 8 out of 10 students began to weep as they encountered the narratives of the disappeared – realizing what they were reading was not fiction.

The experience that Cristina had in Argentina also awakened her to the silence of unawareness. Similarly, her students had been unaware of the migrant population that literally surrounds their university. Cristina feels that as a rule, her students needed to be more globalized – and even more aware of their local community. They were unaware of the university as a place of privilege. The problem, as far as she was concerned, was not only their individual lack of awareness, but also the socially constructed lack of awareness in the insular university community, as an environment that causes and perpetuates silence. Involving them in service learning created a new environment: one which ruptured that silence, so that they could no longer participate in the culture of unawareness in the same way. Thus they could become more aware and contributing members of their own community, and even of a global community. Now they could reflect on the silence of unawareness, shift their frame of reference, and make a conscious choice toward transforming the world around them.

The experience in Argentina changed Cristina profoundly as an educator. She laments that the prevailing culture in universities – to get tenure, to survive the next budget cut – has caused many to lose sight of the vocation of teaching: "creating critically thinking, responsible global citizens." She passionately asserted that after her experiences in Argentina, she could no longer compromise that mission. "I will teach for free," she said, "but these stories must be told, and students must learn to be responsible in their own communities." Paradoxically, the silence of depersonalization and disenfranchisement that Cristina encountered in Buenos Aires led to her own self-empowerment. Her reflection on that silence liberated her from the strictures of academic careerism, and enabled her break through to a renewed recognition of the true significance of her role as an educator. If her teaching is to have meaning, it must lead to the empowerment of her students, both as learners and as actively engaged social participants in the transformation of their world. All of this was brought about by her recognition of and reflection on silence.

REFERENCES

Finchelstein, Federico. 2014. *The Ideological Origins of the Dirty War: Fascism, Populism, and Dictatorship in Twentieth Century Argentina* 1st Edition. Oxford: Oxford University Press.

Guest, Iain. 2000. *Behind the Disappearances: Argentina's Dirty War Against Human Rights and the United Nations (Pennsylvania Studies in Human Rights)*. Philadelphia: University of Pennsylvania Press.

CHAPTER 4

Silence Looking Out and Looking In (Southeast Asia)

Respondent Background
Jarrett Davis
Jarrett Davis's research is a direct outgrowth of his own life. The silence that he encountered growing up is mirrored by the silences that he observes in interviews conducted as part of his fieldwork. The social, cultural and contextual aspects could not be more different, but the silences engendered in each share profound affinities. So too, the reflections to which each gives rise are very similar. For us, the question is: how can we make use of these commonalities to facilitate social change?

Jarrett grew up in the American Midwest in a conservative Christian environment. His mother is a minister in the Nazarene denomination, an evangelical Protestant church in the Methodist tradition. Nazarene doctrine regarding sexuality is very rigid:

> We stand firmly on the belief that the biblical concept of marriage, always between one man and one woman in a committed, lifelong relationship, is the only relationship within which the gift of sexual intimacy is properly expressed.[1]

---

[1] Board of General Superintendents, Church of the Nazarene. "Human Sexuality" (n.d.), http://nazarene.org/organization/general-secretary/human-sexuality.

Not only is this group firmly against homosexuality, according to Jarrett, they equate homosexuality with pedophilia:

> I grew up in a community where "we don't even say the word 'gay.'" For the people I grew up with, "being gay" was synonymous with being a pedophile: we didn't even talk about it.

Because of this stigma – surrounded as it was by silence – Jarrett experienced deep self-loathing as an adolescent and young adult. He was twelve when he first connected the concept of homosexuality with his own experience of sexuality. He recalls, at that time, feeling both devastated and terrified. Because he was attracted to some of his peers (age-mates), he thought that he himself was a pedophile. It was only ten years later, at age 22, that he came to the realization that he was not sexually interested in children: he was simply gay. He regrets now that he "spent so much of [his] life hating [him]self." After earning an undergraduate degree in Religion from a Nazarene college in the USA, Jarrett went to a graduate school and seminary operated by his denomination in the Philippines. The school had the same anti-gay stance as his former college. In pursuit of a master's degree in intercultural communication, Jarrett embarked on a study of identity development in a mission outreach church in the greater Manila area. The introduction to his dissertation includes this trenchant statement:

> The study of identity is significant because it is foundational in the formation of not only who we are, but also what we can become.[2]

---

[2] Jarrett Davis, "Identity and Development: A Case Study of the People of Looban Outreach Church," Asia-Pacific Nazarene Theological Seminary Resource Center. www.apnts.edu.ph/resourcecenter/.../Davis%20Identity%20and%20Development.pdf.

Historical and Geographical Context

Because silence is often concerned with the liminal space between self and other, we thought it important to look at a group of people who occupy a similarly liminal location. Thus, we turn our attention next to the community known as *kathoeys*, or "ladyboys." We will be looking at this group in both Thailand and Cambodia. The term Tagalog word *kathoeys* refers to a transgendered person who is biologically male, but performatively female.

> Many *kathoey* present outwardly, from their teenage years onwards, as entirely female – in terms of hair (often long), dress, cosmetics, manner, gait, gestures, voice, stereotyped personality traits and interests (including vocational). When they speak they employ a female tone and vocabulary, employing Thai word-forms normally restricted to females.[3]

Identification as a member of this group is not, as often in the West, defined by one's anatomy, but rather by a combination of the choice of a particular social role (both in the family and in the community) *and* one's sexual activity: "maleness is defined not only in terms of what anatomy you have, but in terms of what you do with that anatomy."[4]

Kathoeys are seen as a "third gender" throughout Southeast Asia. Although this group represents only about 0.3 percent of the total population of Thailand (and even less in Cambodia), they have a high international profile. This is mainly because of the dual part they play in the tourist industry: in particular their roles in sex tourism and in entertainment (drag shows and beauty pageants). Their visibility on a global platform is significant. It highlights the etic nature of silence, which manifests itself at the periphery between insider and outsider.

Scholars in the field of transgender (TG) studies have identified three bases for the development of *kathoey*: religious, attitudinal, and developmental.[5] Buddhism (especially the *Theravada* Buddhism prevalent in

---

[3] Sam Winter, "Country Report: Thailand." Transgender ASIA Research Centre, Research Papers (2002). http://www.transgenderasia.org/country_report_thailand.htm. Accessed June 21, 2016.

[4] Ibid.

[5] Sam Winter and Nuttawut Udomsak Male, Female and Transgender: Stereotypes and Self in Thailand. *International Journal of Transgenderism, 6, 1* (2002).

Thailand and Cambodia) is largely neutral on the topic of gender. All identity is transient, since the spirit itself moves from one body to another in the course of reincarnation. Gender identity is similarly fluid between incarnations. In addition, one's identity in a current body is to a great extent dependent on karma, that is, on one's actions in a previous life (as we shall see below). Also, and importantly,

> the common belief says there is no escaping from the karmic consequences, everyone has been *kathoeys* at once in previous lives and will be again in future ones, thus *kathoeys* should be treated with compassion.[6]

As we shall see, social attitude towards *kathoeys* differs between countries. In Thailand, the attitude varies between acceptance (in larger cities) and tolerance (in more rural areas). While the stereotype of Thailand is one of openness, especially in terms of sexual matters, the reality is somewhat more conditional. Women have a slightly higher social status than in other Asian countries,[7] and the social distinction between men and women is somewhat less pronounced. Tolerance for difference (gender/racial/ethnic) is fairly high. A 2002 study of *kathoeys* found that

> around 40 per cent... believed that, as a general statement, Thai society was encouraging or accepting of *kathoeys*. Another 27 per cent felt that it tolerated them. Only 15 per cent believed it rejected them.[8]

This is even true at the level of the family.

> Forty per cent of [the] sample said their fathers were either encouraging or accepting when they first made it known that they were *kathoeys*, while 66 per cent said their mothers were... Indeed, around 30 per cent... believed that they were *kathoeys* at least partly because of their parents' influence. Another 30 per cent said the same thing about sibling influence.

---

[6] Janessa Ilada and Ry Mount, "The Third Gender in Thailand". https://maytermthailand.org/2015/04/27/the-third-gender-in-thailand-kathoeys. See also Jackson, 1998.
[7] See Ford and Kittisuksathit, 1994 and Han ten Brummelhuis, (1999). Transformations of transgender: The case of the Thai *kathoeys*. In Jackson, P. and Sullivan, G. (Eds.). Lady boys, tom boys, rent boys: Male and female homosexualities in contemporary Thailand. New York, USA: The Haworth Press.
[8] Winter and Udomsak, op. cit.

In his research, Jarrett has found a "double bell curve" in both Thailand and Cambodia with regard to self-identification as TG. There seem to be two peak periods when this occurs, either at the ages of 5–6 or 14–15, and

> it's quite mixed. Anecdotally, some will say, "my mom started dressing me as a girl...she wanted a daughter...[or] the family saw the person was "soft" and decided "we will package you that way." But then there are others who chose it for themselves – mostly this was the case with those who figured it out when they were older.

Jarrett attributes these two peaks on the bell curve to the two moments at which one begins to be aware of one's gender and one's sexuality, respectively.

These findings lead to the suggestion that the culture itself provides a clear developmental pathway for boys to choose the adoption of a "third gender" identity. Once that choice has been made, hormones are readily available to enhance the female physical characteristics. Sexual reassignment surgery is also available, though not all *kathoeys* take that option, choosing instead to maintain a merely passive sexual role.

The myth of Thai openness towards sexuality does not mean unconditional social acceptance; discrimination exists, especially with regard to housing and employment. But for the most part, *kathoeys* live as women, employed largely in traditionally female occupations (e.g., shop assistants, tour guides, hairdressers, beauticians, and performers). At the time of writing, neither Thailand nor Cambodia had legalized same-sex marriage or accorded full legal rights to *kathoeys*. But progress is evident: in 2016, an amendment to the Thai constitution granted equal rights to male, female, and third-gender people, only the 12th country in the world to do so.

CASE ANALYSIS

Throughout this investigation of group identity, Jarrett began to understand his own identity in a new way. He also began to explore and understand silence better. For Jarrett, the meaning of silence changed as he moved from a lack of self-understanding to a more perceptive construal of his own identity. His attitude toward silence became apparent as he described his research for the anti-trafficking organization Love146. His work brings together the emic and etic perspectives: at certain times he is exploring the respondents' silent internal communication; at others, he is observing how external, cultural dynamics factor into the creation of silence.

> The notion of etic and emic perspectives comes from the world of social science research. Emic accounts describe thoughts and actions primarily in terms of the actors' self-understanding – terms that are often culturally and historically bound... In contrast, etic models describe phenomena in constructs that apply across cultures.[9]

Traditionally, researchers have opted to use either one perspective or the other, and hence employ different principles and methodologies. In an increasingly globalized world, where virtually no person or action operates within a cultural vacuum, a more integrative approach might well lead to greater understanding. Continued exploration of silence should ideally keep both perspectives in play.

The site of Jarrett's postgraduate research takes our own exploration back to its starting point: looking at the significance of silence in relationships which contain an inherent power differential. Jarrett's study was carried out about nine years into a partnership between a large, affluent church (which he refers to as the "mother church") and a squatter community.[10] Adopting Hofstede's framework, Jarrett notes that Philippine culture

> commonly exhibits a high-power distancing between social groups of unequal power... Thus, in contexts with a high power distancing, members of low-status groups accept and expect domination by other

---

[9] Michael Morris, Kwok Leung, Andrew Myers and Bryan Nickels. "Views from Inside and Outside: Integrating Emic and Etic Insights about Culture and Justice Judgement." *Academy of Management Review*, Vol. 24, No. 1 (1999), 781–796.

[10] According to the United Nations Global Report on Human Settlements 2003 ("Understanding Slums"), the community in question falls somewhere between two categories: *iskwater* (Tagalog version of "squatter," referring to a physically disorganized collection of shelters, made of light and often visually unappealing materials, where poor people reside) and *looban* (meaning inner areas where houses are built very close to each other and often in a manner not visible to the general view of the city). http://www.ucl.ac.uk/dpu-projects/Global_Report/home.htm/.

high-status groups, and will often concede power to those of a stronger social identity.[11]

He observes that the strong identification with one's assigned social status is reflected in the self-esteem of the individuals in each group. The low self-esteem experienced by members of the outreach site (and perceived by the "mother church") becomes a central problem in their progression towards self-sufficiency, as they seek to develop leaders.

Three other cultural values are relevant to our discussion of silence. The first is the idea of "Smooth Interpersonal Relations": conducting interpersonal relationships so as to avoid the outward appearance of conflict. This is

> almost synonymous with...the concept of *pakikisama*...[in which one] concedes one's personal likes and dislikes in order to identify with another person or group of persons (at least on the surface) for the purpose of maintaining a harmonious relationship. At its best, this cultural value seeks harmony with others and with oneself; however, it is also possible that it can force one to "go along" with other particular social conventions at the expense of one's own identity.[12]

Pakikisama temporarily silences one's own identity; this can be true either for an individual or for a group, and can have either positive or negative manifestations. Negatively, it can be a tool of oppression. Positively, it can be a unifying force. Jarrett also notes that

> Philippine social structure is organized as an interpersonal hierarchy of relationships that seem to mimic familial relationships. This hierarchy tends to prescribe and maintain the nature of interactions between differing social classes. Those of higher social class or position function in parental roles as caretakers, providers, and educators. As those of lower class or

---

[11] 'Power distance' is defined as "the extent to which the less powerful members of institutions and organizations within a country expect and accept that power is distributed unequally." See Geert Hofstede, *Culture's Consequences: Comparing Values, Behaviors, Institutions, and Organizations Across Nations* (Thousand Oaks, CA: SAGE Publishing, 2001), 98.

[12] Frank Lynch. "Social Acceptance Reconsidered," found in Philippine Society and the Individual, Edited by Frank Lynch (Quezon City: Institute of Philippine Culture, Ateneo de Manila University, 1984), 36. See further, Davis (2011), 101 ff.

position are provided for, they, in turn, owe their loyalty and respect to those who have provided.[13]

Social strata are internalized, and then reinforce oppressive patriarchal norms. The "mother church" was trying to accomplish both a spiritual ministry and a "holistic" one designed to alleviate the consequences of poverty. Jarrett began studying the issues of marginalization and stigmatization that emerged in this effort. He found that the "mother church" was interacting with the outreach church

> just like the [colonizing] Spanish had treated the Filipinos: they were being oppressed, held down, they were not able to self-actualize, the attitude was very patronizing: "these poor, sad babies need rice."

There was a specific meaning attached to silence. It was interpreted as a result of the members of the outreach being inadequate and unable to deal with their lower status.

Ultimately, it became clear to Jarrett that if the outreach mission was to be successful, the group would have to establish its own identity – one which was separate from that of the "mother church," and which was founded on a new self-understanding. The group needed to break the silence imposed on it by the mother church, which it had initially accepted. It had to renegotiate its identity in a way that allowed it to break free of oppressive preconceptions. This is another example of what we earlier called a "toric" action. The act of renegotiating identity was facilitated by an increase in self-esteem which came about through the group's new self-understanding. At the same time, the action itself validated and amplified that self-conception: "this is who we are now; we can do this."

Jarrett had to go through the same process on his own personal journey. The process began with the realization that he was gay, not pedophilic. In thinking about the relationship of the two churches through the lens of social identity theory,

> [a]s I started looking at what it means to have your own identity, I had this self-reflective moment – I've been studying myself!

---

[13] Davis, 2011, 89.

Shortly after this realization, Jarrett went to work with Love146, an international NGO dedicated to the elimination of human trafficking. He recounts that he "still had a lot of internal self-stigmatization." Dr. Glenn Miles, the Asia Director at that time, became a mentor, both personally and professionally, as a social researcher.

> Even though I had already accepted the fact that I was gay – and I knew that was not sick or perverted, I recognized that my work with Love146 would involve research with boys and young men, and I felt compelled to talk to Glenn. It came out almost as a confession: "Given the nature of our work, I think it's important for me to let you know that I'm gay." It was such an awkward moment. He paused with a quizzical look on his face that said: "why is this an issue?" Finally, he looked at me and said, "Great. I'm glad you feel comfortable to talk to me about that." There wasn't any awkwardness – this was a non-issue. This was one of the most powerful and comforting moments for me: total acceptance.

In that moment, silence was comforting. It betokened understanding, connection and acceptance. In a moment of silent acceptance, the silence of self-hatred was shattered.

> I had gotten so used to not being heard for most of my life. I never said anything until I was 22. I had no connections, no girlfriends. I was 22 the first time I told another human being about myself. It was then I slowly – very slowly – began to accept myself.

Jarrett describes two parallel moments in the development of the outreach church. The first occurred when a young man finds his voice, and is then accepted as a leader.

> he is a speechless person (he is shy, speaks very little). He doesn't talk well or keep on speaking, but when he speaks... everybody listens. The leadership [mother church] had one opinion and the youth had another, at that moment this particular youth, one who usually never speaks, spoke up and offered some common grounds on which the two groups could agree. He settled everything with just a few words.

The silence of acceptance broke down barriers for the group. These barriers had been both internal and external: some had been imposed by the colonializing paradigm, while some were a consequence of the group's developmental process. The first step towards breaking down the barriers was to understand what had created them in the first place – and to recognize that being passively and unreflectively silent can often cloud one's perception and obscure one's thinking about the main issue. Transformation of the group's identity – and transformation of their relationship to the mother church – came about when all parties began to realize the true nature of the core issue. In this case, they all seemed to have lost sight of the original impetus. The issue at the heart of the matter was not that the squatter community should try to emulate the mother church, but that all of them should believe in God. This realization led to a renewed understanding of their common goal, which facilitated acceptance and opened a path to transformation.

At the end of his study, Jarrett concludes that the partnership between the two groups will only be successful if they can achieve the kind of mutual closeness that exists between friends: what is known in Tagalog as *barkada*. He cites Michael, a youth leader from the squatter community, who

> believes that real relationships and communication is key in the relationship between the two groups. Michael indicates that the social leveling that took place with his own *barkada* at mother church was a significant part in the process of lifting his own self-esteem. Michael adds that, "if the people of [the squatter community] will become *barkada* with the people of mother church, that boulder [of division] will be gone."[14]

Although he did not explicitly make that connection, in our interview with him, Jarrett described silence in the context of *barkada*:

> There are times that silence is connection. The people that I'm closest to – that I trust – I don't always need to talk with them. Sometimes, we can just sit together silently, and there is connection.

Silence can create space for non-judgmental communication. This is the silence of community, of communion. It is achievable between individuals or between groups, and it can both engender and reinforce a sense of community. As he elaborates in his dissertation:

---

[14] Davis, 2011, 143.

Barkada...refers to a kind of close-knit group with whom one shares a common or equal identity. Relationships in the *barkada* are relaxed, tolerant, and guided by the principle of *pakikisama*. That is, people in the group meet on equal terms and are motivated to minimize the importance of that which holds them apart – in this case, economic status and social influence.[15]

Through his study of the Filipino church, Jarrett developed both a methodological and perspectival framework and a deep recognition of the significance and meaning of his personal journey. He has been able to put both into practice with Love146. Working in Thailand, Cambodia and the Philippines, he has focused on both street-working boys and TG men ("ladyboys") who have been the target of gender-based violence. A striking gap is apparent between government reporting of sexual violence and the research that Jarrett and his team have carried out.[16] Gender-based violence directed at males is often overlooked: sexual abuse and vulnerability is thought to pertain only to women. Love146 looks "at violence against *humans* – evenly – as opposed to one gender or other." In that work, Jarrett observes:

Research is active, attentive listening...People are the experts of their own realities, we respect them as that. We are not the experts on *their* lives. What research in development community needs in this region is respect for respondents. Silence is very important in that work. Listening is really a core value. We encounter silence in a lot of different areas – with social workers, with sex workers, in one-on-one conversations.

Social science research generally entails several steps, beginning with conceptualizing the issues involved. Next comes the creation of a methodological framework. Data collection then ensues. Finally, one analyzes the data from a series of perspectives to cross-verify the validity of the findings. As Jarrett proceeded with his research on the two churches, he deepened his own practice of non-judgmental analysis. For example, in his thesis, he

---

[15] Loc. Cit.
[16] According to 2011 government statistics, in a country of 101 million people, there were only 1,400 cases of child sexual abuse reported – and of those, only 29 people were male. Yet in a random sampling of 55 street-working boys interviewed by Love146, 33 disclosed some form of sexual violence.

even-handedly interviewed constituents of both partner churches. Both of these developments have been facilitated by the fivefold process we outlined in our introduction.

Additionally, in the context of his research, Jarrett has observed six of our seven modalities of silence. The first is the silence of reflection.

> Everywhere, no matter what country or culture, it's a very similar process. They don't respond to it [silence] in the same way. Most people – a very strong majority – are aware of the silence, but they respond to it in very different ways. Empathy comes in all forms, people can manage it differently, at different levels, and some can't handle empathy at all.

He and his team conduct semi-structured interviews of 45–60 minutes. Over the past three years, he has participated in or supervised approximately 500 interviews, in cafés or drop-in centers or on quiet street corners. Sometimes the interviews are done with social workers or other agents who are familiar with the respondents. In all cases, the respondents are told that they can stop the interview at any time if they feel uncomfortable. Talking about vulnerability and violence is never an easy topic. At times, reflectivity has to struggle against a defensive rhetorical posture.

> There is always a lot of talking in the first part of the interviews. There are a lot of words when we start off talking about friends, personal interests, and other light topics, but then we get down into talking about family, relationships, and people who make them feel safe or unsafe...
>
> once we get to that part, the words are fewer and farther in between. It's at this point that you have to pay a lot more attention to body language, there are a lot of unspoken words. We had the same experience with transgender sex workers as with the boys and young men.

As the interview progresses to deeper issues, some measure of self-reflection occurs, and silence becomes more noticeable.

> Although I speak Filipino, in the Philippines I find myself more immersed in body language than in what is actually being said... often the interview just goes silent. In Thailand, this is much more the case, because I don't know what all of the words mean... but the same phenomenon is true: The deeper

and more intimate the topic is, the words become soft and few. Sometimes just one or two words, and there is nothing to fill the silence

The interviewers are trained to manage the silence, to allow for whatever is there to emerge into the silence. The team has learned that silence is often an indication that a trust threshold has been reached. The respondent may be confronting a difficult memory. Or he may be asking himself whether or not it is safe to open up to the interviewer. The silence of reflection then confronts the silence of fear: "Maybe they are asking themselves – 'do I say what really happened? Do I tell the truth?' "

> That is usually where the conversation comes down to the ground, to what is real, more genuine... once you get to the section about sexuality and violence, there are fewer words, but each word has more weight. It's more genuine. With each word you feel you are actually talking to the real person.

Another aspect of self-reflection is evident in the interviews he conducts because of the marginalized space these young people occupy in their society. Members of any minority usually experience some feeling of being "on the outside looking in" at the mainstream culture in which they live. Jarrett himself recounts that he grew up as an outsider looking in to his own life. Non-cis people (those who do not identify with the gender of the body they were born with) experience this to an even greater extent. Jarrett felt that this increased their capacity for self-reflection in and of the silence.

> Most of them are aware of the silence, but maybe not reflective of it. Particularly transgender people got this more, maybe because they're older, and have grown up on the margins. There are really three genders in some countries; the TG have grown up as "not this/not that." The term "ladyboy" is often understood as a kind of "third gender" category. It can be ambiguous, including transgender people, but also sometimes effeminate gay men.

The counterpart to the silence of reflection is the silence of empty rhetoric. At times in Jarrett's interviews, the silence becomes overwhelming for the respondent.

There have been those people who bounce back from the silence, who can't stay with it. They divert it with a joke, recognizing their discomfort. An intimate, quiet silence is too much, they need the comic relief. Other people lean into it.

Occasionally, empty rhetoric even distorts the quality of the data, in terms of measuring the effects of gender-based violence.

> Silence is really important. I have found that, if there is no silence, then either the respondent or the interviewer was not present in some way. In some interviews, especially with street-working children and youth, if the respondent is just freely and glibly talking, you can almost tell there will be nothing genuine there. We check each interview for accuracy by using internal redundancies that we put into the interview questions. If the interview is quick and the respondent is just talking very easily, the redundancies often do not line up, indicating that the interview it's mostly "fluff." We have to put that into the limitations of the research.[17]

Most of the time, however, they encounter the opposite of the silence of empty rhetoric: the silence of genuine presence. Jarrett remarked on the different effects silence can have.

> It can be terrifying (socially awkward) to be with someone and not say anything, there is an innate feeling that you need to perform, to present yourself as something to someone, particularly with someone you have just met, or it can be comforting. The effects of silence are different.

He calls this aspect of silence "restorative":

> You're sitting with the person, valuing the time you're spending with them, just being with them: all of that is all a part of recognizing the humanity of the person in front of you. Being present.

---

[17] "On the other hand, there are some people who are so used to coping with their trauma that they can talk about it freely, there might be disclosure, but they have no internal connection to it."

Jarrett made a distinction between this kind of genuine, restorative presence and the performative self-presentation that is such a large part of the TG experience.

> In allowing there to be silence in the interviews, it's allowing [the respondents] to step away from the performance/presentation aspect, and just be, just sit in what is real, what is in front of them.

He noted that the silence seems to be connected to the emotions aroused by the interview; not so much by the questions as by the process itself. Silence in the interview often allows the respondent to enter into or inhabit the space provided for reflection and recollection. It is not the narration of physical or sexual trauma that brings them to silence – many of them are dissociated from that. Rather, what brings them to the possibility of is the experience of reflection which is facilitated by the silence.

> At the end, we move on to topics like the future, [questions about] well-being, happiness, their hopes and dreams. Particularly in the transgender study, especially in Bangkok, the respondents were thankful. It was shocking was that we had numerous respondents who actually thanked *us*. "No one has taken the time to ask *us* what we feel." You know, we're looking at sex workers in Bangkok: they're tough people. They don't get shaken easily. But towards the end, when we're talking about hopes and dreams, they often they tear up, some start crying. They're moved to have someone caring about their emotional and spiritual well-being. But that only comes after the central part of silence.

The next three modalities that emerge in the context of the Love146 interviews are the intertwined silences of fear, oppression, and hopelessness. Here, some cultural differences between countries become more apparent. In Cambodia, the silence is a result of fear and hopelessness. Jarrett remarks that the level of violence that is directed at the TG community in Phonm Penh is unlike any that he has seen elsewhere. "It is not always safe to be open about who you are, as a transgender person."

Much of the fear, which results in not being able to talk about it, is fear of violence and abuse. Over the 12 months prior to the interviews, 74 percent of TG sex workers in Phnom Penh reported inappropriate physical touch. Forty percent reported a physical assault. Of those assaults,

40 percent were committed by the police: sometimes sexual, sometimes just by way of planting drugs on street workers. Over half of the respondents (55 percent) reported having been forced to perform sexual acts. Out of those, 18 percent recounted rape with physical violence, while 15 percent described things like being forced into group sex, or not being allowed to use a condom.

In Cambodia, most TG are freelance sex workers. This means that they are not connected to a brothel or bar as they often are in Thailand.

> TG sex workers don't come out until after midnight – it's just too dangerous to be out. We saw them being chased on [mopeds], we saw people yelling at them. Once we had to move an interview, because the respondent was afraid of the police in the area. We walked with them to protect them, and then continued the interview in a quieter place.

Mixed with the very real fear of violence is a feeling of hopelessness because of who is perpetrating the violence.

> Where does this discrimination come from, who is responsible? Sadly the top sources are people that children are supposed to be able to trust: 20 per cent was attributed to police, 15 per cent to parents, 16 per cent to other relatives, and 10 per cent to teachers.

The violence and hopelessness is compounded by lack of support from family, social shame and widespread discrimination. This often results in people choosing to be silent, as a coping strategy.

> Particularly in Cambodia, there are high levels of stigma – you just don't talk about it. That's why some of the TG had come into sex work in the first place. They left their family because the fact of their identity was just not up for discussion. In Cambodia, the silence was about stigma, shame, and discrimination; if it's mentioned, it's often met with a dismissive, awkward laugh.

In reaction to rejection by their birth families, many ladyboys form "families" of their own. They live together, relying on one another for support. Factories often hire them as a group. They say things like: "My friends love me, my family does not accept me."

Not surprisingly, these negative feelings are often internalized. In Cambodia, when asked about their thoughts and feelings about themselves, almost half said they feel shame; 42 percent said they felt guilty; 20 percent had suicidal ideation. Just over half – 52 percent – said: "I blame myself..."

In Thailand and the Philippines, the silence is oriented more towards shame and being part of a minority. In Thailand, being a ladyboy is more well defined and talked about more openly. "But there is still there is a lot of silence about being TG in both countries." Ladyboys are still vulnerable to exploitation, and their place in the family and in society is not yet well established. There is still a feeling that "I need to be a proper person who provides for my family and takes my rightful place in the family." A lack of clarity concerning acceptance is even true when the family has been involved in the determination of the child as TG.

These silences can become entrenched in the psyche. Existing social and cultural institutions reinforce conformity to established practices, and provide rationalizations – often unstated – for events. We saw how this dynamic developed in the case of the Filipino church, where a misconception of the core issue led to a closed cycle of conformity, ritualization and emulation that eventuated in an apparently hollow pseudo-identity. Real change was made possible by a re-appropriation of identity through a renewed affirmation of presence. The same can happen for the ladyboys, though this will probably involve a long process.

One cultural dimension that may stand in the way of that transformative process is the influence of *Theravada* Buddhism in Thailand. Therefore, many ladyboys see their situation – both their gender and any accompanying discrimination – as a manifestation of karma.

> In my last life I stole someone's husband, so now I'm a ladyboy. If it's part of your karma, you just accept violence against you; it's your place in society.

In conjunction with this belief, the Love146 interviewers asked what form the ladyboys would like for their next reincarnation, and why.

> 38 per cent said, "I don't care which, but something definite." "I want to be a person – male *or* female." As third gender, they are not given a place in the conversation that is society. They don't really participate, there is a silence – they are not thought to have a right to participate. But if it's your karma, it's not really a battle for you to fight – you just pay your dues.

The final modality of silence that Jarrett observed draws together threads from his interviews and his dissertation. This is the silence that makes space for dialogue, both within and between people. As we have noted earlier in this volume, the more solidly one can establish an equal footing for communication, the more ethical the interaction will potentially be, and we feel that silence plays an important role in making this happen.

Both in the Love146 interviews and in the study of the Filipino church partnership, Jarrett identifies the significance of establishing a relationship of mutuality and authentic caring and respect: a relationship of *barkada* that could be held by and in silence. Such a relationship, we suggest, can plausibly best be formed by an integration of the emic and etic approaches: an understanding that brings together both perspectives.

> I feel like there is a deep and intricate relationship between the etic view and empathy – to be able to stand outside of yourself and look in, in silence, the etic view: to be able to observe what is going on.

As Jarrett found in the process of developing his own identity and in the development of identity for the Filipino squatter church, there was a need for both internal reflection and self-compassion. Both internal and external empathy were integral to transformation.

> Having a genuine interest about their lives made the difference. It was weird for them – no one asks these questions. [Their identity is] assumed, but no one stops to ask how they feel about it. Some almost didn't know how to deal with people asking about the other aspects of their humanity apart from what was underneath their dress. Person to person.

Interestingly, it was difference – the existence of a space between – that made such a relationship possible and meaningful. Difference accomplished a unity that commonality could not. It's a question of transforming rather than conforming. It comes out in both his thesis and his work for Love146. In his thesis, Jarrett brings this out.

> We [Love146] didn't have any TG people on our team. It was interesting that it was meaningful to them that we were a team of cis-people interested in talking to TG people; someone not like them who wanted to hear about them. It was great for them that a cis-gender person could be interested in

their lives... It made the silence a lot more meaningful, someone who is cisgender talking to a TG person: "those are usually the people who don't want to care about me..."

This case study reinforced for us a significant facet of our understanding of the nature of silence as a social phenomenon which comes from and goes to the core of the individual. Sometimes silence is a matter of inner reflectivity: looking inside oneself to see what might emerge. Sometimes it is a matter of observation: of what is on the horizon of one's environment. Sometimes, the most profound silence occurs in the gaze that occurs in the space between myself and another. Looking inside oneself, one can still be aware of the other (the internalized other: the other as agent or subject; the other who is my obligation or partner). Perhaps silence is best recognized as an etic movement, in that you can act ethically even when looking at yourself:

> If we're stuck in the emic – it's all about me, what I need. The etic requires a universal perspective. The silence isn't about my inadequacy – I'm not performing – but it may be about you: step outside of yourself and see where you fit in the silence, and appreciate the silence itself.

References

Costa, Lee Ray and Andrew Matzner. 2007. *Male Bodies, Women's Souls: Personal Narratives of Thailand's Transgendered Youth*. New York: Haworth Press.

Davis, Jarrett. "Identity and Development: A Case Study of the People of Looban Outreach Church." Unpublished manuscript of Master's thesis. Asia-Pacific Nazarene Theological Seminary Resource Center. www.apnts.edu.ph/resourcecenter/.../Jarrett%20Identity%20and%20Development.pdf. Accessed June 22, 2016.

Ford, Nicholas and Sirinam Kittisuksathit. 1994. "Destinations Unknown: The Gender Construction and Changing Nature of the Sexual Expressions of Thai Youth." *AIDS Care*, 6(5): 517–531.

Jackson, Peter and Nerida Cook, eds. 2000. *Genders and Sexualities in Modern Thailand*. Chiang Mai: Silkworm Books.

Jackson, P. A. 2003. "Performative Genders, Perverse Desires: A Bio-History of Thailand's Same-sex and Transgender Cultures." *Intersections: Gender, History & Culture in the Asian Context*, 9. Internet edition available at http://intersections.anu.edu.au.

Nanda, Serena. 2000. *Gender Diversity: Cross-cultural Variations.* Long Grove, Illinois: Waveland Press.
ten Brummelhuis, Han. 1999. "Transformations of Transgender: The Case of the Thai *kathoeys.* " In Jackson, Peter and Gerard Sullivan, (Eds.). *Lady Boys, Tom Boys, Rent Boys: Male and Female Homosexualities in Contemporary Thailand.* New York: The Haworth Press.
Totman, Richard. 2003. *The Third Sex – Kathoeys: Thailand's Ladyboys.* London: Souvenir Press.
Winter, Sam. 2002. "Country Report: Thailand." Transgender ASIA Research Centre. http://www.transgenderasia.org/country_report_thailand.htm. Accessed June 21, 2016.
Winter, Sam and Nuttawut Udomsak. 2008. "Male, Female and Transgender: Stereotypes and Self in Thailand." *International Journal of Transgenderism*, 6(1). http://www.symposion.com/ijt/ijtvo06no01_04.htm. Accessed June 21, 2016.

CHAPTER 5

The Silence of the Unknown and the Unknowable (Guyana)

Respondent Background
Vivian Carlson
Professor Vivian Carlson is a special educator and family development specialist. She is Professor Emerita of the Department of Human Development and Family Studies at the University of Saint Joseph in West Hartford, Connecticut. For the past 10 years, she has travelled two or three times a year to Guyana on the northeast coast of South America.

Professor Vivian Carlson has spent the past 30-plus years working with families where disability is present. As a developmental psychologist, her specialty is working with people in their home environments, assessing their needs and offering suggestions on how to manage the disability of the child in their family. She must also consider the multiple stressors on the family system that often accompany the diagnosis of a disability, including poverty, scarce resources, and social isolation.

Vivian reports that when she began in the mid-1970s, no references really existed for the type of work that she saw as so vital. Plenty of social workers went into homes, and plenty of special educators worked in classroom settings, but combining the two was quite rare. She found herself inspired by her experiences as an undergraduate. The question that she followed was: what happens to people who – due either to some developmental limitation or a genetic disability – do not develop along the usual pathways? She spent a full semester of independent study working in institutions and early childhood classrooms, and subsequently attained a master's degree in Special Education, doing fieldwork in preschools. There she found that by the age of 3 or 4, children have established strong social and developmental patterns, and families have already formed coping strategies and parenting habits. She felt, therefore, that intervention needed to start earlier. At that time, in her region (Connecticut, USA), there was no system for assessing or treating developmental disabilities for children from birth – three years.

Her approach differs somewhat depending on location. In the USA, she can often build a relationship with a family through weekly visits that can go on for several years, up to the child's third birthday. She generally visits Guyana twice a year; there, she is not limited to seeing children, but also works with adults with disabilities. She trains indigenous Amerindian women to carry out her recommendations in the intervening periods. In either case, the uniqueness of Vivian's approach is twofold: first, her emphasis on the person's own environment, and second, her insistence on beginning very early in a child's life in order to focus on shaping how a child is viewed. In addition, she assesses not only what help is needed, but also what and how a child can contribute to his or her environment.

Vivian's attitude towards her work is emblematic of her philosophy. She was raised "by a father who felt a strong sense of duty to others, and that you could not take from anyone unless you also gave." She makes it a point to communicate to families that she learns more from them than they could from her.

HISTORICAL AND CULTURAL CONTEXT

Guyana is a member of the Caribbean trade community. It is home to one of the world's largest remaining tracts of virgin rainforest. It is an English-speaking country of about 730,000 people. Guyana was a British colony from the early 1800s until 1966. In this forgotten corner of the world, many families live in the most desperate of economic circumstances.

Guyana shares borders with Venezuela, Brazil, and Suriname. Its ethnic breakdown reflects its colonial past: people of East Indian origin (descendants of indentured servants from India) comprise 49 percent of its population, people of African origin (descendants of African slaves) make up 32 percent, people of mixed race 12 percent, Amerindian 6 percent, and White and Chinese 1 percent. The people of indigenous heritage live mostly in the undeveloped interior regions. The people of Guyana are extremely poor; in 2013, the GNP was $8,500 per person, making Guyana one of the poorest countries in the Western Hemisphere.

The country carries an external debt that is 40 percent of its GDP. Although the country possesses considerable natural resources in the form of bauxite, gold, diamonds, hardwood timber, shrimp, and fish, the manufacturing base is very small and the national unemployment rate is fairly constant at about 21 percent. Mining is one of Guyana's most important economic activities: sugar, bauxite, rice, and gold account for 70–75 percent of the country's export earnings. Roughly three-quarters of the land mass is forested (rainforest/equatorial jungle); 90 percent of its population lives along the coast.[1]

In a country with such overall high unemployment, it is difficult even to estimate the employment rate of the indigenous Amerindian population. In particular this chapter focuses on the Macushi, who largely live in the jungles and savannahs along the Rupununi River. Most of the Macushi exist on a subsistence level, raising their own food, hunting and fishing with bows and arrows, and supplementing their income with sales of handcrafts. Few of the indigenous youth follow formal education beyond age 12. Most can read English, at least at a basic level.

Health care varies slightly according to location. In the North Rupununi, there are rarely more than two or three doctors in the whole region, which encompasses some 24,000 persons and 22,000 square miles (approximately one person per square mile). However, getting to a doctor from many isolated and riverine communities is often difficult and may take several days. Most villages have a small clinic and a government-trained "health worker" who has less training than an American "first responder."

---

[1] U.S. Department of State, "Guyana". http://www.state.gov/p/wha/ci/gy. Accessed February 5, 2015.

From the beginning of Vivian's work with a family, an attitude of mutual ownership of and responsibility for the work is established. Working in this manner carries a certain risk, but also confers on all parties a shared sense of commitment to improving the situation.

Vivian relates that only twice in 35 years has she ever felt "shut out" of a family system. To her, it is essential to approach people with humility and in a spirit of working together. It is most effective to tell family members that *they* – not she, the credentialed professional – are the experts on their own child and family.

Vivian always enters the home by invitation of whatever program or person has been approached to assess a need. In the US early intervention system, this generally occurs as soon after birth as a challenge or difference becomes evident. In Guyana, however, individuals have gradually learned of "Dr. Vivian" and come to her quietly seeking assistance for their family members. Thus, to some extent, the parameters of the meeting are pre-established: a family has asked for help, and Vivian's role is to determine what help is needed and available, from within or outside the family system.

Prior to an initial assessment visit in the USA, Vivian receives very little information; simply a 20–30-word summary outlining the reason for the referral. No information is given in advance regarding the family configuration, presence of siblings, etc. When she contacts the family for the first time, she asks them what their needs are and what help they are seeking. In Guyana, often the first time she learns about a child is when the family shows up in whatever village she is visiting.

Whether in the USA or in Guyana, the first visit with the family is always primarily about listening. As Vivian puts it, "the first visit is always about hearing the story." The story that is told is often the birth story, especially if something went wrong during the birth that either resulted in the challenges now faced or made those challenges evident for the first time. As she says, "My silence and empathy may or may not give me new information, but people need to tell that story, it's important for them to tell the story." Her silence during the recital of the story sets the tone for the rest of the work together. It expresses her empathy and her willingness for the family to participate (as far as is practicable) as equal partners in the process of diagnosis, assessment, and treatment. Thus, from the very beginning, her first inquiries are established in the space between herself and the family.

Based on the dynamics of the interaction, the first thing that we learnt from Vivian is to make the effort to suspend all activities, including even cognitive ones, in order to create a sense of empathy, of joining. Silence comes from within. It is not based in presuppositions; no processing of information occurs; and all manners of judgment are suspended. Connectivity is established in such a way as to create an equal footing and the boundaries of a shared space. This attitude helps all involved to move to the in-between spaces which have thus been co-created.

A significant nuance should be noted here, between *being attentive* to silence and *paying attention* to silence. Both are conscious acts, but being *attentive* to silence means co-creating a common space, whereas paying attention *to* silence provides room for authenticity and therefore requires interpretative judgment. Both actions (attitudes) are powerful and necessary. The distinction between the two might be understood as the distinction between presence and the ability to witness.

So her first movement is to attention. Only after attention has been recognized does she attempt to bring the information gained to a consciousness of the shared nature of the venture. It is a matter of a conscious co-creation of space. While the family is speaking, Vivian tries to show empathy, to show that she understands where they are by making brief comments. She may try to get some more concrete information about the child's present condition; for example, what it is like to feed him, what his current health concerns are. At the same time, she comments supportively on how well the family is doing with the challenges, providing consistent positive feedback, as well as acknowledging the difficulties that the family is facing.

Vivian stressed that she allows a longer wait time for a response than the culture usually affords. If someone is silent when asked if they need something, she sees that silence as a person trying to organize her thoughts, perhaps to assess the level of the helper's commitment. She allows the silence its own time.

The silent space that Vivian leaves open helps all parties to step away from urgency, even when the point of challenge is to meet an urgent need. This factor has an important effect on the quality of the interaction: calming, engendering patience, reducing the demand quotient. Thinking about bringing what is silent to the center, stepping away from urgency has the effect of re-focusing people on what is important (perhaps allowing what is inessential to fall away). It is not a change in immediacy; rather the focused nature of the joint inquiry removes some barriers, inviting greater immediacy.

All of the recommendations that Vivian puts forward are rooted in the immediate lived context where the challenge occurs. Thus, nothing is outside of the family system from the beginning. Context is everything. Where resources are so limited, everything that is there must be conceived of as available for use, given enough creativity. This factor adds another dimension to the space "in-between": an immediacy within which all parties are operating in common. Being attentive to silence enables this to happen.

The researchers asked if any calculation seemed to enter into the silence of letting people tell their story. Was there ever a sense that people were trying to gauge "what they could get out of it" by crying wolf or exaggerating a need? Vivian could think of only one family (in over ten years of working with dozens of families in the Rupununi) who does that on a consistent basis. They see her as an American who has access to money and power, "so they're always trying to get me to bring them things, get them things, etc."

While Vivian felt that the first two modalities of silence (empty rhetoric and the silence of insolence) were not often found in her line of work, she found the rest of the modalities very relevant to her experience.

The silence of hopelessness and oppression was perhaps the most salient modality of silence that she experiences in her work. The sense of hopelessness and oppression speaks to the most destitute and vulnerable people both in the USA and in Guyana. When she arrives in a village, many people who come to see her don't really know what she can offer. Some come to see an American "because they heard you work with children, perhaps bringing a child with a cleft palate or club foot. These people don't want to tell you anything, they just want you to help in whatever way you can." Vivian is very careful never to promise anything that is either beyond her capacity to deliver or beyond the resources available to the people in their own setting. It would be inappropriate, for example, to recommend maxillofacial surgery to someone living in the Rupununi. It is far better to work with the family to see how they could design viable nutritional, educational, and occupational strategies for a child with a cleft palate. In Vivian's experience, the silence of hopelessness arises because people are accustomed to not being heard or even seen. Because they have no status or power, the very poor are neither heard nor seen, which only perpetuates their lack of status and power. They embrace silence to cope with this reality.

Vivian reports that she has encountered the silence of fear in the same context. For families faced with the challenges of raising a special needs child, there is often a sense that something terrible has happened, but that no one cares. This feeling is universal; a similar sentiment is voiced in Arthur Miller's *Death of a Salesman*, and the same remedy is suggested:

> I don't say he's a great man. Willy Loman never made a lot of money. His name was never in the paper. He's not the finest character that ever lived. But he's a human being, and a terrible thing is happening to him. So attention must be paid. He's not to be allowed to fall in his grave like an old dog. Attention, attention finally must be paid to such a person.[2]

The silence of fear perpetuates the silence of neglect. In Dr. Carlson's experience, attentive listening is the best strategy for overcoming these feelings of helplessness and beginning to build a relationship with families. She finds that asking a very few, gentle questions and allowing for a lot of wait time in the dialogue brings the whole experience to another level. The combination of respect, gentleness, and patience facilitates the co-creation of an egalitarian reality where both the professional and the family bring something to the process. Personally, Vivian does not like using the word "help." Rather, she concentrates on building reciprocal relationships and establishing an atmosphere of mutual learning and working together in this co-created space. This, she feels, is the way forward toward hope.

In terms of thinking about the different modalities of silence, Vivian appreciated that "the silence that makes space for dialogue" comes after the silence of attentive listening. In the silent waiting of listening, her attitude is that if she has something to say, she will say it, but her silence indicates that she is more than happy to wait until the other has something to add.

The first visit, therefore, is already a positive and collaborative effort. In the first encounter, the emphasis is on looking at strengths. On the second visit, one can begin to identify difficulties. In preparation for the second visit, Vivian may ask the family to think about what is most important for them right now, what they would like to work on or improve. During the second visit, then, the family and the professional begin to write goals and

---

[2] *Death of a Salesman*, Act I, Scene 8.

plans together. These don't come from professionals, she stresses, "they have to come from parents, in the parents' own words."

Vivian recounted a recent interaction as illustrative of this way of working. She was at a second visit with a mother of a special needs child. The mother has significant challenges herself. The mother articulated the problems with her child as follows:

> I need her to understand boundaries, to play by herself for five minutes, to not jump on her mother, to be able to focus on one activity at a time.

Vivian would write those goals in the mother's own words. As far as she is concerned, there is little to no value in working on goals that the professional thinks are important, if these are not shared by the caregiver. Despite her challenges, the mother "is right on top of what is needed." Though she may not put her goals in the same words as the professional would do, what the mother says is more important, more salient to the future of the child than the clinical jargon of a developmental report.

In this case, when the report was read back to her, the mother asked, "Why do you say 'J's mother says this'?" Vivian replied that what the mother had to say about the child is the most important information available; because the mother is with her child every day, she is the most important person in the process. No one had ever said this to this mother before (perhaps in an unconscious holdover from paternalistic colonial times?). What emerged in the silent space left by Vivian was the recognition of the mother's unheard voice. It changed the mother's entire outlook on the situation.

Positive encouragement, based on attentive listening and leaving space for dialogue, is given from the first visit onwards. If the child's condition does not improve, then Vivian gets the family to discuss the lack of progress in a non-judgmental way. For example, the physical condition of a child with cerebral palsy can easily get worse if joints are not exercised regularly. Because she has a relationship of mutual caring for the child, Vivian can have a frank conversation with the family to see what the barriers are to the child's progress. Family and professional can explore together what is going on, for example, what needs to be done in terms of positioning or exercise. Together they can engage in problem solving, perhaps calling on other resources external to the family for extra support, if any are available.

Moving into the in-between spaces, as she does, both requires trust and builds trust. Vivian's work provided an almost perfect example of the fivefold process that the researchers outlined with regard to silence.[3] She begins with respectfully paying attention in silence to the birth story or whatever story the family needs to share. She then brings the experience of attention to the family's consciousness, allowing them to feel heard and empowered, perhaps for the first time. She then analyzes the silence, through full engagement with it. She allows the family to set the tone for understanding the silence and their reasons for it. As they move together into action, she inscribes that same silence onto her own thinking, using her clinical skills to diagnose and prescribe, but as far as possible without imposing value judgments, and then encouraging action by helping all parties to consciously act on the basis of their shared reflection.

There is, she says, an almost incremental shift in the silence as the encounter deepens. Certainly, for an experienced professional such as herself, paying attention and bringing what is said to consciousness are instinctual from the outset. Analyzing the silence and inscribing it into one's own action, etc., are steps in a process that builds over time. The most difficult families are those where there is no silence. As a professional, she knows that she needs silence to process and reflect. She can be sensorily overwhelmed by commotion, chaos, noise. In those sorts of situations, it takes her a much longer time to figure out what is going on and how she can get people to engage with her in the in-between space. Thus, paying attention to silence has to occur throughout.

With regard to the fivefold process of silence that the researchers had outlined, all five were generated in this case. She observed a one-to-one correspondence: the interactive nature of the fivefold process fits well with the nature of her work, which is fundamentally interactive. The nature of the silence is not necessarily linear, but it is incremental, at least until she and the family have come to know one another and entered into a relationship of trust. She did not see the five aspects as compartmentalized or as occurring in a stepwise fashion. In her experience, the steps are intermingled and interactive.

---

[3] As a reminder, the fivefold process asks that one (1) pay attention to silence; (2) experience attention: bring it to consciousness; (3) analyze the silence through full engagement; (4) inscribe silence onto one's own thinking; and (5) consciously act on the basis of this reflective process.

Similarly, in her work the seven modalities do not all appear, nor do they appear in a linear fashion. Each family is very different and presents very different circumstances. This can make the quality or nature of the silence different, and sometimes difficult to cope with.

In Vivian's experience, different modalities occur in disparate ways. She felt that the last two modalities – attentive silence and the silence that makes space for dialogue – are aspects that she always hopes and strives for in her work, but if she encounters other modalities – especially silence rooted in fear, hopelessness, and oppression – it may be much more difficult to attain a more positive attitude towards silence.

Dr. Carlson brought to our attention a further modality which our original thinking had not captured. This is the type of silence that begins and ends in humility, which is central to her undertaking. Her work in Guyana has enlightened her to a silence that occurs between people from very different cultures, which she characterized as "the silence of the unknown and the unknowable."

This silence rests on the fundamental human need to find similarities between us. How can we ever know what another's life is like? And why should we bother to try? This silence may indicate that two people are so different that they couldn't possibly have anything to say to each other; the gap between them is too wide. In Guyana, she often experiences this (unspoken) tension: "you're a wealthy American who can afford to travel here, I'm from an ancient tribal culture...how can we ever understand each other?" She works through this silence by utilizing the fivefold process – recognizing its source, reflecting on it, and engaging both parties in the conscious reflection both on the silence and on their common goal, on the gap and on the bridge.

In closing our interview, Vivian asked if any of the steps were meant to encompass a group interaction rather than a dyadic process. She felt that one's own attitude and stance toward silence have a huge impact on the silence that is developed between or among people. The responsibility for the silence lies with the outsider entering the situation, who plays an important role in setting the tone for the interaction. The outsider needs to consciously provide the space for silence as a positive and integral part of the process. One must have a willingness to keep questions open, rather than foreclosing them with the attitude that there is a right answer. One has to keep open the intentional space for thinking and dialogue to occur. This can only happen in the context of a co-created space where all participants engage and interact, moving freely between silence and voice.

References

Abrams, Ovid. 1998. *Metegee: The History and Culture of Guyana*. Pittsburgh, Pennsylvania: Eldorado Publishing.

Carlson, V. J. and Harwood, R. L. 2014. "Precursors of Attachment Security: Behavioral Systems and Culture." In Hiltrud Otto and Heidi Keller (Eds.) *Different Faces of Attachment: Cultural Variations of a Universal Human Need*. New York: Cambridge University Press, 278–303.

Miller, Arthur. 1973. *Death of a Salesman*. New York: Viking Press.

U.S. Department of State. (Guyana.) http://www.state.gov/p/wha/ci/gy. Accessed February 5, 2015.

CHAPTER 6

How Many Layers of Silence Can One Context Hold? (Micronesia)

Respondent Background
Jasmine Mendiola
At 26 years old, Jasmine Mendiola has attained a level of professionalism and poise that few people of her age can boast – gender or ethnicity notwithstanding. Born, raised, and educated on the island, for the past two years Jasmine has been the Assistant Director for an environmental NGO at the southern end of Pohnpei.

The Marine and Environmental Research Institute of the Pacific (MERIP) was established in 1997 "with the goal of providing education and income generating opportunities for rural Micronesians." Despite its small size (a staff of seven, of whom six are local), over the past 19 years MERIP has established itself as an important force for change in the Federated States of Micronesia (FSM).

MERIP's work has a dual focus: applied research and capacity building. Their mission is "to develop and transfer environmentally friendly responsible methods of sponge, coral and clam farming to Micronesian communities."[1] The main thrust is implementing

---

[1] Marine and Environmental Research Institute of the Pacific, http://www.meripmicronesia.org/about-us.

© The Author(s) 2017
N. Billias, S. Vemuri, *The Ethics of Silence*,
DOI 10.1007/978-3-319-50382-0_6

community-based work in aquaculture projects to rural communities with few employment opportunities. Like the rest of the Pohnpeian population, the people whom MERIP serves live "off the land and off the sea." They are primarily fishers with a generally low level of education. MERIP tries to encourage people to apply the skills that they already possess to more sustainable alternatives.

In the recent past (in the early 2000s), Micronesia was the third most productive tuna industry in the world – an astounding statistic, considering its size. As the impact of climate change becomes more significant, Pohnpei needs to seek out other sources of income in order to reduce the stress on its fisheries. At this time, the ocean surrounding Pohnpei is still clean and not overly acidic; it should continue to produce a sustainable income for several years. MERIP's goal is to help the island's fishermen and -women transition to new sources of income for the next generation and beyond.

Since the mainland is fairly mountainous, Pohnpei is not as vulnerable as the Marshall Islands or its neighboring atolls. Thus, despite the fact that they live close to the land and sea, awareness of climate change is only just beginning to take hold among Pohnpeians. Much of the community training that MERIP provides involves introducing the terms and concepts of climate change. "The people in the outer atolls are more aware. The inundation is ruining their crops; high tides and king tides go into their smallholdings. The change is very gradual [on Pohnpei itself]."

Changes in the size and number of fish caught have been noted. Many women, for example, fish with hand lines and canoes in the bay, close to shore. In MERIP workshops, the older women have remarked on how much smaller the fish have become. These changes have occurred in their lifetime, and the circumstances are only going to deteriorate as time goes on.

CASE ANALYSIS

This chapter has no separate section to describe historical and cultural circumstances, because the respondent's milieu is an integral part of the case itself.

Silence emerged in four contexts in this case. All of them are related to time, and to what has transpired over time in a specific cultural context. The first salient silence we observed was related to the influences of past practices on the present: the tension between modernity and tradition and between traditional and changing gender roles. Next, we noted two kinds of silence connected to the present: first, between the NGO world and the values and expectations of the people they serve, and then silence with regard to how certain individuals in the group conducted themselves in dealing with the silence of the others. Finally, silence was evident with regard to the future: silences regarding climate change and uncertainty about sustainable practices.

In each aspect of the interview, we were struck by the live and ongoing consideration of the framework surrounding the work of Jasmine and MERIP. The social protocols within which they operate are at once fixed and evolving, requiring conscious reflection on everyone's part in order to attend to and preserve tradition, while at the same time successfully adapting it to address the needs of present and future.

A great deal of the interview focused on Jasmine's self-understanding: how she came to be who she is within her social context, and how she functions within it. She started to recognize and deal with silence from a very young age. She describes herself as a very vocal person, and feels that her personality often demands that she voice any concerns that she encounters. She was raised to be vocal.

Both sides of her family contributed to the development of her voice. Both her parents had a traditional upbringing,

> but they were very open-minded and welcomed change and [new] ideas, especially when it meant improvement in certain necessary areas. This included adopting Western ideals and lifestyles, especially Western knowledge and even values. They were actually very traditional. They had fairly high titles, and they were the *Nahnmwarki*'s (high chief) "right hand," to the point where they would house-sit the royal residence when the chief and his wife would go off island. They participated in all traditional activities, and held certain Pohnpeian beliefs and values. I believe they used what would be best for every situation, either traditional or non-traditional, whatever they felt would be the best fit to reach a certain resolution or result. So they were a very good mix of both traditional and non-traditional characteristics.

In light of our theme, it is fascinating to note that the tribal structure in Pohnpei actually includes two sets of chieftains: a "talking" chief and a "silent" chief. The silent one is the more powerful; the "talking" chief fulfills more of a facilitative role in decision-making. Jasmine's parents were closely connected to the *Nahnmwarki* (silent chief) of her clan.

She reports that her father was raised in a very traditional Pohnpeian family; his father was quite authoritarian, and did not speak to the children much. Children on Pohnpei generally have a closer relationship with the mother. They respect the father, but the father is traditionally more distant and reserved. Children are taught to not speak their minds or voice concerns; doing so is interpreted as rebelliousness. Children are expected to comply uncomplainingly with their father's decisions and directives. Jasmine reports that her own father grew up with the realization that this traditional state of affairs "did not work for him" – he was acutely conscious of the silence of his father, and of the gap that existed between his father and himself.

On her mother's side, two strong female role models informed and shaped Jasmine's development. Her maternal grandmother was the first female senator in the FSM congress. Her mother received a Western education and worked outside the home. Thus, Jasmine was raised in an atmosphere which understood the cultural values around silence, and which provided models for succeeding within those cultural parameters. In addition, Jasmine's family environment provided conscious and critical reflection on the social norms of her culture. "[Pohnpeian] women are traditionally silent, but my mother had a voice, and my father respected her voice. Growing up, I saw that and I liked it."

Jasmine considers herself very fortunate to have found a partner who is also not completely "traditional" in his outlook. While many Pohnpeian men still reject women as equals, Jasmine's partner is much more egalitarian. She attributes his attitude to his exposure to Western cultural norms as a result of having spent four years in the US military. The couple have a seven-year-old daughter, who is also being raised to speak her mind.

Jasmine is dedicated to not being silent, but rather to being able to express herself freely. She explains:

> Pohnpeiian culture is very traditional. Women still mostly wear skirts, not even long pants, and certainly not shorts... Women are mostly expected to be silent... It is not normal in our traditional culture for women to be out "in the field"; women are either stay-at-home mothers or office workers.

Thus, simply by virtue of her position, Jasmine makes a very clear statement about her own relationship to tradition and to silence.

Jasmine studied marine biology at the College of Micronesia-FSM and has been with MERIP for three years. She describes her first days at MERIP as requiring a very specific attitude towards silence which is instructive of the Pohnpeian value system in general. She explains that

> the meaning of silence is respect: 90 percent of [the reason for silence] is that foundation of respect. This value is reflected in the way we greet people and even the words we use to address them. Pohnpeian is a very complex language... there are three levels on which you could address someone: very familiar (as to a partner or friend); formal (as to, for example, a teacher or a friend of your father); and a third level which is used only in addressing chiefs.

When she began at MERIP, Jasmine feels that both she and her coworkers made a conscious choice to be largely silent with one another. For her part, she was trying to learn, to pick up as much information as she could. On their part, they were using silence to show their respect for her, despite her youth and gender.

Over time, she reports, the other staff members have come to treat her more as a superior, but largely the staff functions as a team. However, she is in a managerial position and supervises other staff, including men older than herself. While her position is in direct conflict with the norms of traditional culture, she feels that her colleagues respect her and her position. She feels that she has had to "learn to be equal with them." In her opinion, it is important to understand everyone's perspective, in order to build a better team.

She also feels that the way she speaks to them is important, that she show that she is "one of them" rather than exercising authority over them. In this way, she replicates to some extent the role of a mother in Pohnpeian tradition. She says: "They tell me things they wouldn't tell my boss, that they would be hesitant to bring up to him. They see me as a bridge." She appears to be quite comfortable inhabiting this position.

The question of perspective is also critical to her effectiveness in community building. When discussing strategies to manage climate change,

> I need to be one of them, to see it from their perspective. If we say "Can you cut down fewer trees?" it's like saying "You should cut your paycheck in

half." If we are going to take something away from them, we have to give them an alternative – and that is what we are doing. We don't have million-dollar projects... but if we can incorporate other grantees, that will grow. The key is to be one of them.

Yet another facet of silence is revealed when interacting with visitors from the government or partner organizations such as USAID. On those occasions, she says, most of the talking is done by herself or the director. The others are silent except when asked something, or if the discussion involves their area of expertise. When interacting with foreigners, it is often considered rude to participate in a discussion.

MERIP's capacity-building programs demand that Jasmine confront silence in very direct ways. Context is extremely important in determining who may speak. Pohnpeian culture

> is still very male-dominated. So the context does matter. Younger people and women don't say much or make decisions, and we sort of accept that... [whether and when I speak] depends on who I'm talking to, [whether I am] in the office or [at a] traditional feast. If someone of higher civil status is speaking, you do not. It's all about respect. Silence is an important norm in Pohnpeian culture.

MERIP's work focuses on encouraging traditional groups to look beyond their current income streams and diversify in ways that will be more sustainable for the environment and also provide long-term strategies for employment. The work is inherently difficult; from the outset, it involves directly challenging a number of deeply held cultural and social values.

For example, one of the unpopular messages that MERIP needs to communicate to the islanders is the damage that dependence on *sakau* root wreaks on the environment. *Sakau* is an essential staple of Pohnpeian culture. *Sakau* (kava) root is the foundation of a mildly narcotic beverage that is an indispensable aspect of all social events.

> When we go and do campaigns, we ask them to take care of the environment. That conflicts with how people are earning their livelihood, cutting down trees for *sakau*. So they don't like us – they depend on that income.

Sakau is now used beyond its traditional role in feasts and other events – it is now a commercial product, sold at markets (bars), and has thus become a big source of income for many people. For both traditional and modern reasons, therefore, asking people to consider a change in their *sakau* consumption is not an easy conversation – but it is a necessary one for the healthy future of the island. How can such a difficult conversation be opened? Here, several aspects of silence emerge:

> When we approach [villagers], we want to be accepted. We don't introduce ourselves: the older men of the village introduce us. We have certain ways of going about things. We are very subtle. We let them say what they want to say first. They may say, "We're concerned because you're asking us not to make a living..."

The conversation begins with the silence of resistance, suspicion, fear. For their part, the MERIP staff need to maintain silence out of respect if they hope to get any sort of hearing or buy-in at all. A dance of silence ensues:

> We have to wait until they give us a chance. [At a certain point, the elders] say, "We will ask you now to give your presentation." Then we stay silent while they give their feedback.

Meanwhile, another facet of silence appears. In these group meetings:

> As a young woman, I don't speak at all. I am silent except when directly addressed – the traditional system is very strong. Whatever the leaders say, the people will follow. So I have to work within the system. [When given the opportunity,] I explain that we are there to help them to find and begin to produce an alternative that is going to be more environmentally sustainable.

MERIP always asks the men to invite their wives and daughters to these presentations, and much of Jasmine's work involves talking with the women. The group is often asked to break into smaller groups in order for different perspectives to be heard: men, women, and youth. They are asked: "what are the greatest threats in your context?"

It is also important for the MERIP employees to stay silent at this point of the process. "We try not to give them ideas, we want to hear the answers from them, their original answers." MERIP emphasizes that everyone's answer and perspective is important, and that the villagers have important local knowledge. Unfortunately, they don't always feel that is the case.

They often feel that their contribution is not relevant. The conversation displaces their experience into a western context:

> We are introducing Western concepts like climate change, and Western terms like acidification. They have [important] knowledge, but they don't know that it's important information to us.

Then, of course, personal attitudes towards silence are also present. Younger women are more silent, as are those who are not well informed or well educated. In one workshop, one woman was married to the head of the Micronesia Conservation Trust. "A lot of the women looked to her to answer on their behalf, they weren't open to voicing their ideas themselves."

It is not possible for MERIP to hold capacity-building workshops for women only.

> If we held one just for women, there would be a lot of talking! The women would be much more comfortable, much more open. The men would disregard it, though... a few men have more respect [for women's ideas], but most men still regard women as not being decision-makers.

How is the fivefold process that we initially suggested represented in Jasmine Mendiola's experience? Her context presents an intricate complex of interconnected and multi-layered silences. In each of the previous cases, silence was encountered through interaction with the other – often a novel, sometimes even an exoticized other. As such, the process entailed bringing an encounter with a silent other to conscious awareness. In this case, silence is encountered from the inside out: it is the context within which the individual begins and within which she must establish herself. The work here is to bring the internal encounter with silence to consciousness.[2]

Because it is ongoing and dynamic, the fivefold process does not unfold in a linear fashion. Jasmine is continually surrounded by many modes of

---

[2] The discussion of silence within groups in this chapter owes a great deal to Robin Clair's 1998 book *Organizing Silence: A World of Possibilities*. In that work, Clair explores both external and internal forces which may bring certain members of a group to silence. As Clair points out, movement toward silence is often a matter of choice. We will see this same dynamic operative in the next two cases as well.

silence, and all of her life she has been engaged in recognizing, interpreting, and responding to silence. As her personal and professional life has developed, she has begun to inscribe silence onto her conscious thought, which then informs her ongoing practice.

The interactive fivefold process has influenced Jasmine's thinking about her position as an NGO worker. Recognizing these aspects of silence in her daily life, Jasmine acknowledged that she has a crucial intermediary role. She represents neither the government (the new order) nor the tribal ("traditional") system. This liminal status allows her a certain freedom from influences of both structures. As a representative of MERIP, she has a well-specified role, which confers the right to present and to participate in discussions and decisions.

> I was raised in between traditional and Western values. When I was growing up I usually stayed away from traditional practices; they're not comfortable for someone like me. But as I got older I started observing the way things are done here. Now I understand it more, now it makes sense to me.

During the interview, Jasmine reflected on what she has learned about herself in carrying out this role. As a child she had always been interested in science, and in diving. Recognizing these interests, her mother suggested that she enter the field of marine biology. Jasmine reports that she loves her work, and is excited to be able to combine both passions in one position. She recalls that when she was in college, she was one of only four women students in a class of 20. Of the other three, one is in Hawaii continuing her studies, while the others work in banks or offices. Jasmine now frequently takes students from her *alma mater* on field trips. She is excited to report that the number of female students has been growing every year.

She had always wanted to use her scientific knowledge to work in the NGO world. After graduation, she worked for a time in an office job at the Australian Embassy, and then for the Western Pacific Tuna Commission, which regulates tuna fishing for the region. However, that position turned out to consist mostly of entering data from fishing vessels, rather than data analysis. So she was thrilled to be offered a position with MERIP, where she had been for three years at the time of our interview.

Much of the work that she undertakes with MERIP reinforces an emphasis on women being part of the workforce. While many of their projects don't involve women at all, in 2015 MERIP received a USAID grant which had a focus on gender equality. Now they are trying to communicate that focus. Of the seven MERIP staff members, two are female. In addition, their community enterprise projects now employ five female "farmers" – farming giant clams, corals, and sponges.

In her current role she feels that she herself does not use silence enough:

> I have learned that I should use silence more often – I have learned that sometimes it's better to stay quiet, just to avoid miscommunication or misinterpretation. If I voice something, my intent is to say what I think, but often it is taken the wrong way, especially by people who are not open-minded. If I voice a concern, it is taken as defiance, not as an opportunity to consider a new idea... so sometimes it's just better to stay silent.

Her natural inclination is to speak her mind, but over time she has recognized that doing so can sometimes get in the way of achieving goals, because it gives rise to conflict.

> Recently I came across a nice quote: "Arguing with a fool only proves that there are two!" Often, arguing is a waste of time. In many ways I've learned that it's better to stay silent just to keep things peaceful – even if I plan to do the exact opposite of what the person thinks.

At times conflict is unavoidable. Jasmine is conscious of maintaining a balance between judicious self-chosen silence and silence that is enforced from without:

> In most of my personal experience, it's very important to voice concerns regardless of how people will take it. I'm responsible for what I say, not for how [someone] will choose to interpret it. Some people will hear what they want to hear; they hear only what they think you are against.

And of course, effective communication is not only a matter of what one says, but of the tone in which something is expressed.

> I've also learned the importance of how you word what you say, and your tone. In most ways, it's best to voice what I want to express. I can't hold it in. I always say to myself afterwards, "I should have said that..." Better to say it and be happy with that.

As she has grown into her role at MERIP, she has developed a greater sensitivity to and understanding of using silence in ways that are appropriate to her milieu.

> My job involves a lot of interaction with very traditional communities, [so] I've learned when and how to speak as a young female. The difference is how I say things and how I act. I need to respect [others] in a Pohnpeiian way. If I'm speaking to someone who has a traditional title, I can't say "Do this, do it this way!" No way! I have to say, "Do you mind helping me with this? Don't you think maybe we could...?" In my current job, I've had to learn to do that.

On a more personal note, Jasmine reflected that silence is also often a matter of individual style and interpretation. She contrasted her own behavior with that of two of her sisters. One is quite reserved and does not voice opinions often. When she does, however, it is clear that she has thought deeply before speaking. Another sister is very outgoing, "she can say anything on any subject...and strike up a conversation with almost anyone." Jasmine's own style falls somewhere in between: when she has something to say, she will say it. She noted that even if her more reserved sister has an opinion, she will often stay silent.

With regard to her quieter sister, Jasmine brought up another important fact of silence. She feels that her quieter sister shares more with her than she does with other people, primarily because

> She knows it will stay with me. I won't judge her, we understand each other. I'm always there to be the ear for venting. Because I listen...a lot of people listen just to respond. Sometimes we don't need a response; we just need someone to listen. Silence is important there, more important than a response.

Although Jasmine's experience of silence is very different from those presented in the previous chapters, some striking parallels emerge. Not only can the fivefold process be clearly discerned, each of the seven modalities of silence is readily apparent. This case suggests that these modalities exist universally, despite variances of culture and ethnicity. They are recognized and managed in a manner unique to their cultural context, and over long periods of history, customary practices have evolved to deal with silences.

For instance, intricate conventions regarding speech and silence are set up to avoid the silences of insolence and empty rhetoric, and to govern the interaction of clan members, from the "talking chief" on down. Some of the cultural protocols which we discussed above reflect the manner in which the silence of hopelessness is managed: women have no difficulty in breaking their silence in the absence of men. They find their voices to speak to other women when an occasion is presented. The silences of fear and oppression are experienced by young people in the context of both family and clan. These silences are not seen as absolute, but breaking the protocols requires courage and support. The silence of attentive listening was exhibited by Jasmine as she endeavors to "be one" with her NGO team and the people she is trying to serve. Finally, she embodies the silence that makes space for dialogue in "listening without responding" to her sister.

The day after our interview, Jasmine sent some further reflections on silence in Pohnpeian culture. During the interview, she had emphasized the value of respect as the basis for the cultural norms around silence. Upon further reflection, however, she wanted to add a cautionary note:

> While all this silence in my culture is founded upon respect, and I honestly think this is a *fact*, because it has kept order, diplomacy and friendships till [the] present day, in some ways silence is not always the best way to deal with things.

She then spoke about some of the undesirable repercussions of silence, most notably, domestic violence (against both women and children) and suicide. Cultural norms which reinforce women's compliance to their husbands and children's deference to their parents' wishes can – and often do – have negative results. For example,

> domestic violence is not considered abuse here. If a man hits his wife, it is usually assumed that the woman had done something wrong, mainly something disrespectful to him and hitting her is to remind her where she stands within the family unit. The same goes with child abuse: here it is not seen as abuse, it is discipline. While in many cases the causes behind both scenarios are actually true (a woman disrespects the husband or the child is being taught right from wrong), to me this does not justify physical violence.

At its most extreme, the silence of fear can be fatal:

> Many suicides are due to familial issues that are not voiced, [people are] afraid of voicing their troubles/concerns because it's just not accepted and if they do, they will get "disciplined." Many of these cases involve teenage pregnancy. It is almost taboo to talk to your parents about birth control or any sex education, so teenagers end up making uninformed decisions. And holding all their troubles inside, it builds up and they have nowhere to turn and are afraid of judgement, [so] they go with the fastest way out – suicide.

REFERENCES

Clair, Robin P. 1998. *Organizing Silence: A World of Possibilities*. New York: SUNY Press.

Federated States of Micronesia. http://www.nationsonline.org/oneworld/micronesia.htm. Accessed June 19, 2016.

Marine and Environmental Research Institute of the Pacific. http://www.meripmicronesia.org/about-us. Accessed June 19, 2016.

CHAPTER 7

Who May Speak? Who Must Be Silent? (Australia)

Responded Background
Julian Gorman
Julian Gorman is a Research Fellow at the Institute for the Environment and Livelihoods at Charles Darwin University (CDU) in Darwin, Northern Territory, Australia. His primary research is on natural resources-based livelihoods. Julian has advanced degrees in botany, resource and environmental management, and geographic information systems. For the past 16 years, his teaching and research have focused on natural resource-based enterprise in the Northern Territory (NT).

Julian began working with Indigenous Ranger (IR) groups when he started at CDU in 1999. At that point, most people in Aboriginal communities were involved in a government-funded Community Development Education Program or a "work for the dole"-type program. The latter laid great emphasis on training indigenous people for "real jobs" – that is,, jobs with an outcome – that conform to Western ways of thinking about work.

One major difficulty with this emphasis, however, was the fact that very few such jobs actually exist in the townships. The program became better known as the Community Development *Employment*

Program (CDEP) as the emphasis shifted from education or training for real jobs to a welfare-based employment program.[1] This iteration of the CDEP operated a variety of projects around communities. Initially, in each of these projects, people worked for four hours a day. However, even several small government initiatives did not provide enough jobs to keep people gainfully employed. Over the next ten years, this idea led to the development of the IR program, which was offered to members from each clan.

Until 2007, the ranger program was part of the CDEP and run by the Land Councils, and linked closely with the "Traditional Owners (TOs)." TOs are decision-makers specific to each clan estate. Those Aboriginal people who had been displaced and wanted to claim back their land through the High Court needed to provide evidence that they had maintained a connection to country and culture. In the absence of written records, status as a "traditional owner" is established on the basis of being known (or one's family being known) to other indigenous people.

Beginning in 2007, the government decided to dissolve the CDEP, and consultations were held with Aboriginal communities about ending the program. After a change of government, it was decided to restructure the CDEP. As of 2016, the transition to the "New Start" program is nearly complete. When it seemed that the CDEP would be abolished entirely, the Australian government set up money to pay wages to IRs and to provide them with sick and holiday pay as well as other entitlements. The aim was to encourage the development of "real jobs" and help people to move from dependence on the government to self-determination, control over land, and eventually, economic self-sufficiency. Although well intentioned, this shift created a new layer of complexity, which was manifested in yet more variants of silence, as we shall see.

---

[1] Community Development Employment Projects (CDEP), Department of Families, Housing, Community Services and Indigenous Affairs Publisher Department of Families Housing, Community Services and Indigenous Affairs, Canberra, 2013.

Over the past decade, Julian has come to appreciate the merits of working as a practitioner alongside indigenous partners, not merely as an academic in a research "silo." He worked on secondment from CDU with the Northern Land Council as a Wildlife Enterprise Development Facilitator and combined this with teaching at CDU and other research projects. For example, he partnered with the Indigenous Land Corporation to explore opportunities and barriers to wildlife-based enterprise development; and with the Australian Centre for International Agricultural Research, looking at floriculture in the NT.

One significant project has been with the Rural Industry Research Development Corporation (a governmental organization). In this regard, he has been seeking to collaborate with indigenous partners to investigate the commercial potential of native wild plants and animals, or to provide them with fee-for-service land management assistance. Specifically, he has focused on developing a model to expand cultivation of a native plant (the Kakadu or "billy goat" plum, *Terminalia ferdinandiana*) into a profit-making industry.

The idea is to grow the Kakadu plum industry with Aboriginal involvement and ownership. This is being done through a not-for-profit industry partner, Kindred Spirits Enterprises, to set up a cooperative venture. Tradition Homeland Enterprises acts as the central processing hub. It can receive fruit from regional collection hubs and deal with processing, quality control, and product development. The collection hubs are businesses in themselves which are owned by someone in the community. In Wadeye there is a women's center which runs the collection hub; they handle and sell on between 4 and 6 tons of fruit each season. This center pays community members to harvest the plants (80 percent of the pickers are women), as well as paying people to handle the fruit. The other component is composed primarily of IRs (not necessarily from the local area), who work in the processing hub and liaise with the government employees. They act as intermediaries between the Aboriginals and outsiders. "The women do the groundwork, and the men come in to run the business."

HISTORICAL AND CULTURAL CONTEXT

Nearly one-third (31.6 percent) of the current population of the NT are Indigenous Australians.[2] Over 50 percent of the land is under Aboriginal ownership, and customary harvest of wildlife (plants and animals) makes up a significant component of the Aboriginal economy.

Indigenous people have the lowest economic status of all Australians.[3] In 2006, only 55 percent of Indigenous people nationally over 15 years of age were participating in the work force.[4] This includes those in mainstream employment, participating in the workforce in some way (under government schemes) or unemployed. It has been suggested that unemployment rates could be as high as 90 percent if various government-funded community development programs (such as CDEP) were not taken into consideration.[5]

The peoples of the NT, like Aboriginal peoples all over the continent of Australia, have an extremely close relationship to the lands on which they live. This relationship has been complicated, altered, and distorted by the influence of the colonizing forces over the last 200 years. During this time, there has been considerable fragmentation of the tribal structure and the totemic organization of the various clans. In addition, there has been further destabilization of traditional kinship arrangements, both because of (sometimes forced) movement or displacement of people from their land and because of inter-tribal and inter-racial marriages that might not have taken place had the Aboriginal ways of life never been disrupted.

Although white people have only been in the NT since the 1820s, their impact on the Aboriginal peoples of this area has been immense and

---

[2] Australian Government. "Closing the Gap," http://www.aihw.gov.au/closingthegap. Accessed June 6, 2016.

[3] J. C. Altman, "The Howard Government's Northern Territory Intervention: Are Neopaternalism and Indigenous Development Compatible?" *Centre for Aboriginal Economic Policy Research.* Topical Issue No. 16 (2007).

[4] Australian Bureau of Statistics. "A Statistical Overview of Aboriginal and Torres Strait Islander Peoples in Australia," http://www.hreoc.gov.au/social_justice/statistics/index.html. Accessed: June 6, 2016.

[5] Tony Abbott, "Grassroots Capitalism," (paper presented at the Indigenous Employment Conference, September 25, 2002, Federal Ministry for Employment Services and Workplace Relations, Canberra).

devastating. Tribes or clans have nearly always undergone a drastic dispossession. Some were forcibly displaced from their land by mining companies or large farming concerns. Some were allowed to remain on the land, either on farm stations (ranches) or in the mines, if they agreed to work for subsistence wages. Later (beginning in 1877 and continuing until the mid-1930s), several groups of Christian missionaries performed another type of displacement by separating children from their families of origin. Most of this was done forcibly (from educational or health concerns), while at other times families were persuaded to part with children by the promise of rations. Government-sanctioned forced removal of Aboriginal children was not formally abolished until 1973.

By 1910, the government had carried out an effective program of segregation by enforcing the creation of compounds or townships to contain the indigenous population. There was widespread disregard for the integrity of indigenous customs or values. The emphasis was on "converting and civilizing" the Aboriginal people to fit into the colonizers' worldview. Aboriginal people were only granted Australian citizenship in 1967, at which point they were granted equal protection under the law, including wage parity.

All of these artificial settings have played havoc with the traditional groupings. Today, a Township (as the compounds came to be called) might be organized around a central regional support hub. Thus a dozen or more groups may be found in one township – as many as 3,000 people. The township may be made up of a number of more-or-less cohesive clans, but there is no guarantee that the clans in question had any original claim to the land on which they are now living. Each township has a different history, a different composition, and a different understanding of how it came into being. Little written information is available. Much of the history is a matter of oral tradition, which becomes less reliable as older inhabitants die out. Younger people don't necessarily have the continuity of knowledge to appreciate the importance of either the geography or the history of the old, traditional boundaries. Family stories are also being lost. Among many other problems, the lack of understanding of origins often leads to gang warfare in the townships.

In addition to the loss of connection with their original land, and restrictions on their ability to travel freely, another serious difficulty for the indigenous people has been the loss of their original languages. The language spoken in a township is often an amalgam of "pidgin" English, flavored by decades of intermingled tribal languages. No one common language exists to bind people together.

Given this history, it is extremely difficult to bring a fragmented group to consensus on shared outcomes. It is often not even possible for government officials to know precisely whom they are speaking with. The composition of any group is decisive when it comes to the nature of the silences, as shall be seen below.

CASE ANALYSIS

One of the salient aspects to be considered in this case is a direct result of the historical background. The tumultuous history of the indigenous peoples of the NT over the past 200 years has made the dimensions of space and time particularly significant, in the following way. Over time, the people have experienced a radical and decentering change of space. They have experienced destabilization and displacement, a significant lack of written records, and the choice of the colonizing language as the primary medium of communication. Through all of these factors, the change of space impacts the nature of silence. History becomes confused, as short-term amnesia in reaction to individual trauma becomes long-term communal memory loss. Thus on the one hand, people may retreat into silence, while on the other, silence becomes diffused. It may, in fact, become so fragmented that either the meaning of the silence disappears altogether or it becomes deeply engrained as a mode of thinking. In either case, the historical context has a profound impact on the quality of the silence.

When asked how he had observed silence in working with these groups on enterprise development, Julian recalled his initial "shock" at what seemed to be an utter lack of interest on the part of the people. Often no one would turn up for a scheduled meeting, either to share ideas of what they wanted to do or to discuss what they hoped the government could do for them. It evolved that there were many complicated reasons for this behavior.

> At first I worked through [Indigenous] Rangers. The first step was to determine: "whose country is this?" We needed to talk with them about why we're here, then set up a community meeting, and get people to come forward with ideas. Only a few people would show up. So we had to use our existing connections.

Julian began by interacting with Rangers whom he had known through his previous wildlife enterprise work.

> A lot of the time it wasn't the [offer of] money that made the difference: it was a matter of connection – maybe going back 20 or 30 years. Connection was really important. [For the indigenous people] being able to work as a family group, participating in the transfer of knowledge, etc., was more important than money.

Some of the resistance he encountered was based on recent history.

> They had experienced several government interventions which often involved a constant flow of state and federal public servants coming into a community to "improve conditions" and involved endless meetings and discussion with TOs that often eventuated in no action. People didn't want to be "TOLD." So some of the reasons for their silence was that people were fed up with continuously changing policy. There was a perception that it was "all talk."

A much more potent factor had to do with the composition of any group that might choose to meet with him. Although to an outsider, a group might seem to be homogeneously indigenous, it would be more appropriate to say that in most cases, there is a homogeneous nomenclature for a heterogeneous group identity (which we might refer to as a "mixed" group). People were displaced and repatriated at many different times and in many different ways. Thus, today a whole range of identities exist to express a person's relationship either to land or clan, in terms of kinship affiliation and/or affinity with a particular part of the country.

Within this range of indigeneity, there is a certain amount of tension between some IRs and TOs. Some of the "IRs" come from other parts of the country – they are Aboriginal people, but have no primary relationship with or claim to the land on which they are now living. The 2007 shift from CDEP to welfare-based funding had one unintended consequence: in many places this change resulted in less connection between the Rangers and the rest of the community. This happened because only limited positions and wages were available for a certain number of Rangers, whereas before (on CDEP) a much larger number of community members were involved.

Another area of confusion is the fact that often Aboriginal townships have a number of different clan groups residing in them. Some are the land owners of the surrounding country and other property further afield. As a result, different TOs have different levels of authority about activities in different areas. Thus, inadvertently the wrong people could be included in a discussion which they could not comment on.

The subtlety of the differences between these categories has a profound influence on the way silence is manifested, observed, and analyzed. At least two important values need to be discerned here.

The first has to do with the internal silence of the group. Meeting with a "mixed group," composed of both IRs and TOs, was a very different experience from meeting with a group consisting only of TOs. A "mixed" group would not have any shared sense of internal silence. First, the non-local members (some Rangers and outsiders) would be happy to "plug in the gaps" of silence. With a fully indigenous group, one often encountered the sense that something was being held back, not being said. The problem is that an outsider (whether that be a government official or a Ranger) would never be able to tell what kind of a group it was, and this would never be made explicit. The group's silence was a manifestation of a shared projected identity.

Outsiders (including some Rangers) who are invariably uncomfortable with silence, ask questions and push for clarification. In so doing, it may be perceived that they have no sense of respect for the group. The indigenous people may be offended by this apparent lack of respect, but this feeling would never be expressed openly by the TOs. This is another aspect of silence that simultaneously expresses a feeling of superiority and of alienation: "I am not going to humiliate you by commenting on your lack of culture, but you are beneath my contempt."

The second salient aspect of silence is that in a "mixed" group, Rangers have to demonstrate their respect for TOs by observing silence in a very particular way. According to Indigenous protocol, they have no right to speak on certain issues. Decorum dictates that they have a duty to be silent in these matters. For non-indigenous people (outsiders), Rangers are central as go-betweens in the process, both because of their facility in several languages and in their knowledge of both Aboriginal and non-Aboriginal constructs. Thus, they may (have to) be silent in a meeting, but will be much more forthcoming outside of it.

There was often an unspoken conflict between the Traditional Owners and the Aboriginal Resource Center. People would talk to you afterwards. There was less silence outside of the big meetings, when the Traditional Owners would be controlling the conversation.

This control was manifested by a certain form of silence, but it extended much further.

The Owners had to give permission for anything to happen. People didn't have the authority to go to the next step. There was a definite hierarchy, not only who could talk, but also who could make decisions. Nothing can be decided in one community meeting. It might take a long time before people come back to you with a decision. It's not just a matter of one Traditional Owner – there might be five or ten who need to be consulted. Outsiders come in expecting to come away with a plan, outputs, etc. That's just impossible.

The cultural gaps between Aboriginal and non-Aboriginal people extend to both ontological and epistemological constructs. This is not only a matter of a common language, but also of a common worldview with regard to values.

Walking the value chain together is often key to understanding the process. Business acumen is part of everyday life for us, but Indigenous life is completely different. They don't really have a concept of a market. So much is informal, with no thought of legislative oversight.

Let's turn again to the modalities of silence we proposed in Chapter 2. As we reviewed the transcript of our interview with Julian, we realized that this case brought us to a new level of understanding the nature of our project. It is relatively straightforward to see how the framework which we had established at the outset was manifested. However, what we had not expected was that the epistemological framework which we had constructed might already be latent in the ontological context of the situation. That is to say, certain types of silence arose out of the evolving interactions. We did not superimpose the structure onto the events. Rather, the events themselves created the silences, which then demanded an ethical response.

The modalities of silence that we are focusing on are readily apparent in this case: the silence in response to empty rhetoric ("it's all talk, talk, talk"); the silence of insolence when encountering cultural misunderstanding; the silence of hopelessness, oppression and fear from a people who have experienced 200 years of poor treatment from colonizers who now seek engagement as partners in joint ventures.

As for the more positive modalities of silence – the silence of attentive listening and silence which makes space for dialogue – these became apparent when we asked Julian to reflect on the influence on his own work of his encounters with Aboriginal silences. How had these experiences changed him as a practitioner? Did he remain silent himself about what he had observed?

> I'm now less vocal in terms of going in and setting things up. Now I find out who to talk to, first. [And] *they* decide who should be involved. I don't know the right people, but they do. As I become more involved, I realize the complexity.

The silences involve more than hierarchy – the nuances extend to the ownership and use of totems, to the linkages that exist between and within clans, even to who can handle which species of which plants. The silences that permeate the process are a manifestation of the difference between value systems. The white people are looking at project outcomes, bottom line success, ecological sustainability, economic self-sufficiency. For the Aborigines, on the other hand, maintaining the cultural complexities is far more significant than any financial gains that might accrue in a business enterprise. For example,

> there are "poison cousin" relationships – [where people] can't even look at or sit in the same car or room with one another.

In the Aboriginal worldview, cultural protocols are extremely important in "caring for country." A good example is the commercial use of cycads. In east Arnhem Land, *Cycas orientis*, is extremely abundant and there is a large national and international market demand for Cycas species. Many cycads are listed under the *Convention for International Trade of Endangered Species* and trade is restricted to try to reduce poaching and unsustainable harvesting practices. The population numbers for this particular species are massive, and a sustainable harvest program could be set up with confidence. However, it is not the ecology that is the main concern here, but rather cultural belief. The Aboriginal people in this area believe that at a specific point in the plants' development, the souls of their ancestors may take up residence in the plants. Since they might contain the spirit of a relative, they can't be sold off-country. You might get silence by talking about the wrong species in the wrong place.

> Another example of a market opportunity that clashes with a cultural value is the matter of reptiles, either in the pet industry or in the food industry. A certain animal might be totemic for a certain clan; imagine proposing to a clan whose totem animal is a frog that there is a large and lucrative market for frogs' legs.

Some people believe that [animals] should be born, live and die in the same country – will not be open to moving them for "off-country" use. You might encounter hostile silence if you propose a commercial use for something of great cultural significance.

Most significant is the fact that in the Aboriginal worldview, everything is divided into two halves which fit together into a whole. This means first, that everything is interconnected, and second, that everything – and everyone – is part of either one group or the other. People, animals, plants, and even the different winds are classified in this way.

> Everything in the Yolngu Aboriginal world is divided into two moieties: *dhuwa* and *yirritja* – you're either one or the other, [the classification] governs who can work with what species.

In all of these cases, silence is due to the ignorance of the Other, and how the other forms and/or perceives groups. The silence is usually either a response to or a result of the misunderstanding of one another's culture in the consultation process.

Julian Gorman's experience with Aboriginal enterprise development is an intriguing example of the fivefold process at work. In order to attain outcomes that would be successful for both worldviews, he found that he had to first, pay attention to the silences he encountered, then reflect on the experience and analyze it through full engagement. At that point, he had to inscribe silence into his own thinking. "It's the personality of a facilitator. You want to involve everyone, not to sit back and listen. But that doesn't work." He then began to consciously act on the basis of this reflective process.

This case is a vivid reminder that whilst we had elaborated an abstract construct regarding silence, almost as if it were a monolithic concept, in point of fact, silence is a dynamic and fluid process which is always responding within a unique context to very specific triggers. Therefore, paying attention to silence begins with recognizing that silence is co-created by all the participants of an interaction. Bringing silence to consciousness, then, means maintaining vigilance regarding the interaction itself. It's important not to lose sight of the process because of anxiety over outcomes.

Suppose I am talking, and the other is silent. I can continue to dominate the conversation, to get my point across, to move us towards an outcome. Or, I can stop and reflect: why is the other silent? What internal processes are going on? What is the quality of our interaction? What role am I playing in the construction of this silence? This is much more than simply "leaving room for the other": it is creating a space for something new to emerge between us.

In order to achieve this, I need to inscribe silence into my own thinking – as a partner in the dynamic co-creation of silence. This will require that an "expert" shift her attention to creating the optimal conditions for communication, rather than merely bridging the silence with words or imposed solutions. If I am not able to adjust my own thinking to meet the specific context, I may only perpetuate the stagnation of our blocked communication.

The last aspect of the fivefold process became apparent when we asked Julian to describe his "success stories." There have been a few areas which have engendered great community engagement and enthusiasm. In each case, it was a matter of finding a common point of contact between the "white" values and the Aboriginal values. For example, the Rural Industry Research Development Corporation wanted to explore a commercial forestry project. They had to think: "How are we going to start? We can't just say 'Let's cut the trees,' a top-down approach would never work."

Julian decided instead to begin by creating a database ranking the commercial ability of different native species. These rankings were weighted for all of the possible factors that might impact upon the commercial success along the value chain taking into account cultural and social, ecological, economic, legislative, logistic (harvestability and storage/production) factors. The weights contributed to an overall score which determined the ranking of a species. This process was just a starting point and was run through with community members to ensure weightings were accurate.

There are certain land management actions or wildlife products that never fail to get a good turnout at meetings. One of these is fire.

If you talk about fire, you get a great turnout. Aboriginal people associate it with cleaning, with sustainability. There are different types of fire that people within clans are allowed to start, and different tasks that certain people are allowed to perform. All of this reveals and reinforces community structure and status.

So, Julian invited the community to a fire to present his database. He explained the process he had used to rank wildlife products for commercial use, and asked for their input. He then brought up individual species for ranking, getting input from the community about the correct weightings for the various aspects (especially cultural and social), and shared with them the weightings that the community might not have much knowledge about (commercial, legislative, logistical). Thus the community itself played an important role in choosing which species ranked the highest and should be targeted for further feasibility studies. One was a native honey bee called Sugarbag.

[The honey] is a great food, sweet (and there is not much of that in the bush). Unfortunately it often gets raided, and virtually never gets to the market. People are interested in it largely because to get it you have to go out to the deep country, which is a very important opportunity. And it's culturally significant – they have a great connection to the product – songs, stories, connections between people, old and young.

In the course of that project, some species were identified that might not have ranked highly, but that people were still interested in pursuing. Initially there was silence around the reason for this. It was assumed that the reason for the silence was because this particular species was a common staple food for the Aboriginals. Harvest of this species was time consuming and it had a low market value (taking one hour per kilogram to harvest). But the harvest activity brought people together, and it is likely that they were interested in the produce in part because of the social aspect. It came out that in addition, they were aware that the plant has medicinal properties, for example for treating skin cancer – no small consideration in a desert culture. This may have been a driving factor that had not originally been communicated. It may have been because the plant had considerable commercial value. Much of this type of information had been previously taken from the Aboriginals before any partnership agreement had been put in place, so they were wary about sharing it. This property had not shown up in the "market research"; they were altogether silent about it because they were protecting that knowledge for themselves.

This last point brings us to the very core of what this case taught us. Ultimately, our aim is to create strategies for ethical interactions, by proposing ways of attending to silence. The people needed to protect their indigenous ecological knowledge because they did not trust their government "partners." The historical context meant that the interaction was already broken at the beginning. Among many other things, their silence was an indication of mistrust.

In order to bring about social change, trust must first be established, and, if broken, healed. If that happens, the nature of the silences can shift from negative to positive. Our contention is that this transformation can only occur if the process of conscious reflective action is continually communicated in these interactions. There will always be a plurality of silences in each context. The task is not to eliminate these silences, but rather to recognize their co-created nature, and work together to understand the profundity of the lessons contained therein.

REFERENCES

Altman, J. C. 2007. "The Howard Government's Northern Territory Intervention: Are Neo-paternalism and Indigenous Development Compatible"? Topical Issue No. 16/2007, Centre for Aboriginal Economic Policy Research, Canberra: Australian National University.

Australian Government. 2011. *Community Development Employment Projects (CDEP) Program Guidelines 2009–12.* Canberra: Department of Families, Housing, Community Services and Indigenous Affairs. http://www.fahcsia.gov.au/sa/indigenous/progserv/families/cdep/.

Australian Government. 2007. *Development Employment Projects (CDEP) Program. Program Guidelines 2009–12.* Canberra: Department of Families, Housing, Community Services and Indigenous Affairs.

Clair, Robin P. 1998. *Organizing Silence: A World of Possibilities.* New York: SUNY Press.

Convention for International Trade of Endangered Species. https://www.cites.org/eng/disc/species.php. Accessed May 31, 2016.

LaFlamme, Michael. 2007. "Developing a Shared Model for Sustainable Aboriginal Livelihoods in Natural-Cultural Resource Management." In L. Oxley and D. Kulasiri. (Eds.). *MODSIM 2007 International Congress on Modeling and Simulation.* Canterbury, Australia: Modeling and Simulation Society of Australia and New Zealand.

CHAPTER 8

Individual, Collective, and Strategic Silences (USA)

Respondent Background
Herbert Ruffin II
Herbert Ruffin II is Associate Professor and Chair of the Department of African American Studies at Syracuse University in northern New York State. Founded in 1870, Syracuse has a total student population of just over 23,000 (of whom 7,000 are postgraduate students). Syracuse is a private, coeducational research university.

Professor Ruffin's research interests focus on African-American US history and Africana studies. He is interested particularly in the history of African Americans in the US West, in social movements and in community development. Herb's research focuses on the experiences of African Americans in the American West, as they sought opportunities for employment, housing and education. The communities of African Americans in western states were significantly smaller than in either the South or the North. Therefore, their experiences were in many ways very different from – though often parallel to – those of African Americans in either the "Jim Crow" South or the urban North.[1]

---

[1] "Jim Crow" refers to a practice or policy (official or unofficial) of segregation or discrimination toward Black people. The term comes from the name of a song sung in minstrel shows in the 1830s.

To be sure, unconstitutional racial segregation laws were often passed by individual states (such as in Oklahoma in 1916). But many actions that occurred in the western states went largely unnoticed by the general American population. One infamous example was the Tulsa race riot of 1921, where the most affluent Black community in the USA was decimated by violence within 24 hours. Herb concentrates on exploring the strategies which small African-American communities in the western states have developed to combat the structural racism that persists throughout America today.

In the course of completing an undergraduate degree at the University of California at Santa Cruz, Herb spent a year of study abroad at the University of the West Indies in Barbados. He returned to California with the idea of heading to UC Berkeley for graduate study. During his year abroad, however, the Proposition 209, known as the California Civil Rights Initiative, was passed by a vote of 55 to 45. This new law was an extremely important piece of anti-affirmative action legislation; through it, California became the first state to make it illegal for public (that is, state-run) universities to consider any applicant's race or ethnicity in the admissions process. It also had a direct personal impact on Herb.

Prior to that time, universities had encouraged the development of more diverse student bodies by actively recruiting minority candidates. Since state-run universities are much less expensive for state residents, they were often the first choice of minority students. With the passing of Proposition 209, the diversity of these institutions plummeted. For example, in the fall of 2015, the racial demographics of UC Berkeley's incoming class were: Asian, 32 percent; White: 29 percent; Latino/Chicano: 12 percent; and African American: 3.8 percent.[2] Professor Ruffin recalls: "The feeling was that the heart had been ripped out of them after that vote had gone down. Many students would come up to me and ask me if I was an athlete." Given the climate created by the new law, Herb opted to

---

[2] University of California Berkeley, Office of the Chief Financial Officer, Office Planning and Analysis. Accessed June 16, 2016.

apply to a private university in Southern California. He completed his PhD at Claremont Graduate School in 2007. The communities on which Professor Ruffin focuses his research do not fit neatly into conventional categories. Therefore, they provide space for a new understanding and interpretation. This circumstance has encouraged him to move beyond what he knows of the usual patterns and paradigms of the African-American experience. The "peculiarity" helps to focus his attention on what is new and different about these situations, and the reactions to them. In addition, what has been the role of silence in their history.

HISTORICAL AND GEOGRAPHICAL CONTEXT

African Americans currently make up approximately 12 percent of the total population of the USA, roughly the same percentage as the number of Hispanics/Latinos. (Interestingly, nine out of ten Americans think that the population of African Americans is much higher, approximately 33 percent.)[3]

Despite the fact that there was an African American in the White House from 2009 to 2016, unfortunately racism is alive and well in the USA, some 50 years after the Civil Rights movement. Following the American Civil War (1861–1865), several amendments to the US Constitution had given African Americans equal rights under the law. Slavery was abolished in 1865; citizenship was awarded to the formerly enslaved in 1866; and voting rights were guaranteed to all, regardless of race, in 1869. After the Civil War, many African Americans moved to the urban centers in the northern states, where the atmosphere was less overtly racist.

Yet from 1896 to the 1950s, racial discrimination was set into the structure of American society, in what was known as the "Jim Crow" era. During this time, individual states were able to pass laws that contradicted or circumvented the federal laws, and many Southern states did so. The doctrine of "separate but equal" ensured that African Americans faced widespread and systematic discrimination. As long as it could be

---

[3] See, for example, Joseph Carroll, "Public Overestimates U.S. Black and Hispanic Populations," Gallop News Service, June 4, 2001. Accessed June 8, 2016.

demonstrated that equal services (housing, education, etc.) were provided, segregation did not explicitly violate federal law, although as time went on, it became apparent that segregated education did not ensure equality of standards.

From 1954 to 1968, a series of federal legislative acts gradually began overturning discrimination and enforcing integration. The first landmark ruling in this regard was the 1954 Supreme Court decision *Brown v the Board of Education*, which outlawed segregated education. The Civil Rights Act of 1968 was meant to guarantee equal opportunity in employment and guarantee fair access to housing. Fifty years on, however, while outright discrimination is illegal, structural racism remains problematic both in the mindset of mainstream America and in the systems and infrastructure of its social programs. Recently, some African-American leaders have begun to speak of this phenomenon as the work of "James Crow":

> "We come as the children of Dr. King to say that we are going to face Jim Crow's son," Sharpton said. "Because he had a son called James Crow, Jr., Esquire."[4]

These leaders contend that Jim Crow never retired from the struggle for White supremacy; rather, he went to law school to learn new ways to oppress Black people legally, such as through voter suppression and other forms of discrimination.

The effects of structural racism can easily be seen in a few startling statistics. For example, even though African Americans represent only 12 percent of the total population of the USA, they are incarcerated at nearly six times the rate of Whites. According to the Federal Bureau of Prisons (2016), 37 percent of all prisoners were Black and 33 percent were Hispanic. Furthermore:

- African Americans now constitute nearly 1 million of the total 2.3 million incarcerated populations.

---

[4] Herb Ruffin II, "Which Came First, Jim or James Crow?: *De Jure* Racial Discrimination Revisited," in Sherwood Thompson (ed.), *The Encyclopedia of Diversity and Social Justice*, ed. Sherwood Thompson (Lanham, MD: Rowman & Littlefield Publishers, 2015), 448–452.

- Together, African Americans and Hispanics comprised 58 percent of all prisoners in 2008, even though African Americans and Hispanics make up approximately one quarter of the US population.
- According to "Unlocking America," if African Americans and Hispanics were incarcerated at the same rates of Whites, today's prison and jail populations would decline by approximately 50 percent.
- One in six Black men had been incarcerated as of 2001. If current trends continue, one in three Black males born today can expect to spend time in prison during his lifetime.
- 1 out of every 100 African-American women are in prison.

One might contrast those statistics with the current percentage of non-White Americans enrolled in higher education. While roughly one-third of all US citizens attend some form of tertiary education, only 20 percent of those are African Americans. A Brooking Institution report (2015) suggests that this circumstance may be influenced by the fact that while segregation no longer exists officially,

> [t]he school system remains highly segregated by race and economic status: Black students make up 16 percent of the public school population, but the average Black student attends a school that's 50 percent Black...the average Black student also attends a school at the 37th percentile for test score results whereas the average White student attends a school in the 60th percentile.

In economic terms, the racial disparity is even more stark. Unemployment rates for Black Americans are double those of Whites (8.8 versus 4.1 percent). In 2013, the poverty rate among Black Americans was three times that of White Americans (27.2 versus 9.6 percent).

Finally, according to the Brookings Institution (2013), even if Black families follow certain "norms" in an attempt to attain middle class status (completing high school, maintaining full-time employment, and having children after the age of 21), their actual rate of successfully reaching middle class status is far lower.

> White Americans are significantly more likely to demonstrate all three norms than Black Americans: about 65 percent compared to 45 percent. Rates of high school completion are similar, but Whites are significantly more likely

to have a full-time job and to delay childbearing than Blacks... Among those who follow all three norms, Blacks are significantly less likely to reach the middle class than Whites who do the same. About 73 percent of Whites who follow all three norms find themselves with income above 300 percent of the federal poverty line for their family size, while only 59 percent of Blacks who adhere to all three norms fare equally well.

Case Analysis

Wherever silence appears, its meaning is conditioned by a number of factors. The first factor is the event itself. The second is the interpretation made of that event, both by the individual and by the groups with which the individual identifies. A third factor is the impact the event has on the interaction of the individual in both the groups to which he belongs and the groups to which he wishes to belong. A fourth consideration is the importance of what happens over time: how does the event change the individual? How does interpretation of the event change over time? Lastly, what does silence mean to the individual in his social context, where his actions are always to some extent influenced by social norms? Reflection on all of these facets of silence contributes to one's understanding of silence. The modalities which we have identified already exist within and are integral to the phenomenological structure; all demand attention.

Herb outlined for us several forms of silence that he has observed in his research. One common trait that they all share is a deliberate and tactical disjunction between appearance and actuality. While silence may seem to be passive or merely accommodating, in fact, beneath the surface, a great deal of purposeful and strategic work is being undertaken. In Herb's words,

> people may appear to be silent, but it may be noisy behind the lines. It may well be that in that silence, people are coming to understand the different tactics that are needed... to get change to happen.

The contention of this volume is that silence needs to be an important part of any planning process; planning helps one to, as Herb said, "know exactly what you are trying to accomplish." Silence assists the process so that one can "think strategically and negotiate with administration, community members, [forging] broad networks."

One therefore needs not only to recognize that silences exist, but also to understand the underlying purposes behind each type of silence. The "end result" of such a process is the recognition of a new phase. But that is not the end of silence.

Perhaps one might usefully think of silence as an activity in terms of a Hegelian dialectic: a dynamic progression punctuated by periods of reflective silence, each of which gives rise to the next. One task, then, might be to explore what new silences emerge into thought as a consequence of the preceding silence, which can then give direction or shape to the next phase of understanding or action.

The silences that Herb describes are both evolutionary in nature and context-specific, as they integrate simultaneously many responses to injustices. The evolutionary and integrative nature of silence described by Herb is dormant in the initial stages of considering an event. It may remain so for a long time. At some point, either an event will occur or a personality will emerge through which the silence is broken, and a new stage of the process arises. The new event shatters the silence, and in so doing releases a new series of opportunities for reflective silence. Thus, silence never completely disappears. It is an integral part of the evolving process.

Herb illustrated the evolutionary and integrative nature of aspects of silence through several examples related to both the history of the Civil Rights movement and the contemporary Black Lives Matter movement. Throughout, it is possible to recognize illustrations of the silence of people who are deeply entrenched in the atrocities of racism.

Herb observed two primary expressions of silence in this context. The first is a strategic, purposeful silence which gathers people together on broad-based issues. A remarkable example of this type of silence was the "quiet" work of A. Phillip Randolph, who preceded Martin Luther King, Jr. as a national advocate for Black equality. From the middle of the First World War to the 1960s, Randolph worked to accomplish the goals of African Americans by framing the problem as existing well beyond racial lines: as an economic issue rather than "merely" a racial one. Something of an unsung hero today, Randolph was invited by the Socialist Party to run for vice-president of the USA in 1940 and was vice-president of the AFL-CIO in the 1950s. He has the dubious honor of having been the first African American to be put under surveillance by J Edger Hoover and the Federal Bureau of Investigations.

Randolph was instrumental in achieving two great strategic advances in the struggle for racial equality for African Americans. Both were accomplished by a quiet and dogged persistence, using general/industrial unionism and Gandhian tactics for social change. The first tactic involved collective struggle for workplace democracy and self-management.[5]

> In 1925, as a trade union advocate, he successfully organized the Brotherhood of Sleeping Car Porters (BSCP). By 1929, they became the first African American union to be incorporated into the American labor movement with a semi-autonomous charter within the American Federation of Labor (AFL). Eight years later, the BSCP unprecedentedly became a completely autonomous Black union within the AFL and the Pullman Company with collective bargaining power. In 1925, as a trade union advocate, he successfully organized the Brotherhood of Sleeping Car Porters (BSCP). By 1929, they became the first African American union to be incorporated into the American labor movement with a semi-autonomous charter within the American Federation of Labor (AFL). Eight years later, the BSCP unprecedentedly became a completely autonomous Black union within the AFL and the Pullman Company with collective bargaining power.[6]

Randolph's second use of Gandhian non-violent tactics was the part he played in the opening of the defense industry to Black workers in 1941.[7] Shortly after the end of the Second World War, Randolph also facilitated the desegregation of the US military. Prior to that time, work in defense and munitions factories was restricted to White employees.

These actions were "silent" in that they were carried out without either fanfare (before, during or after) or widespread public involvement. Randolph began by building a collective base of Black Pullman porters

---

[5] Unionization and Mass Marching wer adapted from the European trade union movement of the 1910s.

[6] See Herb Ruffin II, "A. Phillip Randolph," in *Icons of Black America*, ed. Matthew Whitaker.

[7] Actually he had been using Gandhian non-violent tactics since the late 1920s, to intersect mass protest and direct action politics during the Brotherhood's battle for collective bargaining as an AFL trade. From this, "big bluff politics" was invented. The most famous use of this politics was during the March on Washington movements in the 1940s and 1960s.

and Black domestics. Then, in conjunction with the Brotherhood of Sleeping Car Porters, he built tactical alliances with labor leaders, legislators, and business leaders as socialist with a mass Black political base. By framing issues in a political economic framework that had a direct and systemic impact on African Americans and working people, the Brotherhood argued that the resultant social and labor changes would benefit all working people. By 1937, this coalition forced both the AFL International and the Pullman Company to recognize the BSCP as an international charter – a first for a Black trade union.

Twenty years before the famous March on Washington led by Martin Luther King, Jr., Randolph "placed ads in newspapers requesting that 10,000 blacks gather to March on Washington. Their slogan was, 'We Loyal Negro American Citizens Demand the Right to Work and Fight for Our Country.'"[8] The purpose of this event would have been to demonstrate against the fact that Black workers did not have access to jobs in the defense industry. Such an event would have led to domestic unrest just as the USA was becoming heavily involved in the Second World War. It would also have undermined the claim of the USA to be a democratic nation; that we were not fascists or imperialists. According to Herb,

> Randolph did not organize on a day-to-day basis. To this end, he leaned heavily on the administrative talents, independent thought, and grassroots presence of senior Pullman porters such as Milton P. Webster and C.L. Dellums. They formed the core of a national network of Pullman porter administrators/advisors whose strongholds were in Chicago, Detroit, Pittsburgh, St. Louis, New York and Oakland. As a labor leader, Randolph had an intense fascination with European Immigrant Unionism and Marxism. He always strove to balance these ideas in the struggle for racial equality. There were many others louder than he was. He was great at doing the executive [actions which are so] important for creating [change]: [his work] is silent, but it speaks very loudly.[9]

---

[8] Ruffin, "A. Phillip Randolph," 737.
[9] See Ruffin, "A. Phillip Randolph" for a fuller understanding of this issue.

The Gandhian quality of Randolph's silence can be illustrated by a quote from the Mahatma (1938):

> In the attitude of silence the soul finds the path in a clearer light, and what is elusive and deceptive resolves itself into crystal clearness. Our life is a long and arduous quest after Truth.[10]

Silence is needed to find a clear path to future action. Silence can be powerful in developing tactics but may not lead directly to power. Prior to the 1960s, Black nationalists like Marcus Garvey and the United Negro Improvement Association collaborated with a broad range of activists against European imperialism. They were also collaborating with Randolph. Most world leaders fall from power once their goal is achieved. It is therefore not a surprise that Randolph fell out of favor as a leader as the Black Power movement began to emerge.

The 1960s saw a shift away from a strategic "politics of accommodation," from "respectability politics," which sought to make changes to the system from within the system. This shift was marked by the rise of two types of Black nationalists. Both emphasized Black political-economic and social-cultural empowerment. On the one hand, cultural nationalists emphasized Blacks understanding their negritude through regeneration of pride in the creative capacities of African Americans, as distinct from mainstream artistic expression. On the other, revolutionary nationalists like the Black Panther Party for Self Defense emphasized political-economic empowerment and community control through the direct fight against an inherently unjust system through their survival programs and on the streets of Black urban America. Combined, both groups stopped looking at mainstream America for solutions, and turned inward to create and then expand "survive and thrive" programs.

Many African Americans became silent in the face of the Black Panther movement. During the period of their greatest influence (1966–1971), the Black Panthers were impatient of those African Americans who wanted to toe the line within the system while working for integration. For them, progress was moving too slowly. The Black Panthers believed in direct action, organizing people to take action onto the streets, working with more urgency and greater visibility. (After 1971, they took their politics back into the electoral realm, for example, as board members of the City of Oakland and Alameda County, and as electoral advocates for

---

[10] Mahatma Gandhi, "Silence and Action," *Harijan*, November 26, 1938.

Congressman Ron Dellums, Oakland Mayor Lionel Wilson, and Bobby Seale.)

The second expression of silence that Herb referenced relates more directly to the development of the Black Lives Matter movement. Randolph, Newton, and Seale were particularly effective because they made alliances with non-Black groups to bring about social reforms that benefited African Americans. In a parallel fashion, the Black Lives Matter movement has marshaled strength by looking within and across Black groups beyond its initial focus. Their tactics were not new; the collaborative work of the founding members of the Black Lives Matter movement echoed the collaboration of the SNCC, CORE, and Black Panthers.

In fact, the now-famous "Black Lives Matter" meme was created by three queer Black women from the western United States with very varied social agendas.[11] Alicia Garza of Oakland, California, focuses on the rights of domestic workers. Patrice Cullors lives and works in the Los Angeles area on criminal justice reform, particularly as a racial issue. Opal Tometi is an immigrants' rights advocate in Phoenix, Arizona. Together, in 2013, they founded the Black Lives Matter movement in response to the acquittal of George Zimmerman for the murder of an unarmed Black youth, Trayvon Martin. According to their website "The Feminist Wire":

> Black Lives Matter is an ideological and political intervention in a world where Black lives are systematically and intentionally targeted for demise. It is an affirmation of Black folks' contributions to this society, our humanity, and our resilience in the face of deadly oppression... designed to connect people interested in learning more about and fighting back against anti-Black racism.

It is important to note here that, as commonly encountered in contemporary media, the phrase "Black Lives Matter" does not necessarily represent a monolithic group. The hashtag (#Blacklivesmatter) and meme was appropriated (without permission) from the group's founders, and is now used by a plethora of groups with similar aims, as well as by the original organization – similar to the use of the term "Black Panthers," which originated with The Lowndes County Freedom Organization in 1965

---

[11] The term "queer" here is the term which those individuals use to identify themselves, as distinct from binary hetero norming.

under the direction of SNCC. As such, it is representative of a movement rather than of one specific group. (Use of this phrase is, in fact, emblematic of one of the forms of silence that Herb noted in our interview – of which more will be said later.)
Herb feels that the group's

> organizational structure builds on the legacy of earlier reform campaigns, including the Civil Rights/Black Power movement, Pan Africanism, Africana womanism, the LGBT movement, and the Occupy Wall Street movement, while using cyber-activism to promote its agenda. Specifically, Black Lives Matter puts the feminist theory of "intersectionality" into action by calling for a united focus on issues of race, class, gender, nationality, sexuality, disability, and state-sponsored violence. It argues that to prioritize one social issue over another issue will ultimately lead to failure in the global struggle for civil and human rights.[12]

The original "Black Lives Matter" project has undergone extraordinary development in four short years. By August 2015 – just over two years from its inception – the founding group had grown to incorporate at least twenty-three national chapters around the USA, and several chapters in Europe, Africa and Latin America. The following year (between August 2014 and August 2015), it organized over 950 protest demonstrations calling for social justice, especially – but not solely – addressing the issue of police violence against Black people. In November, 2014,

> Black Lives Matter activists joined with other grassroots organizations like Oakland's BlackOutCollective to disrupt successfully holiday season shopping in [malls and Walmart stores in] San Francisco, Boston, Chicago, Memphis, New York, Seattle, and Washington, D.C. These organizations used the busiest shopping day of the year to remind shoppers and larger communities that the issues of police brutality, access to proper health care, housing discrimination, poor education, immigration reform, racial disparities in median wealth, and the prison industrial complex had to be addressed by the entire nation. These demonstrations, as with all Black

---

[12] Kimberlé Crenshaw, cited in Taylor Hawk, "Intersectional Feminism: What It Is and Why We Need It for a Truly Gender Equal World." https://www.theodysseyonline.com/intersectional-feminism-gender-equal-world (Retrieved 10.7.16).

Lives Matter protests, were intentionally provocative in order to draw attention to issues that were continually ignored by most non-Black people.

This action embodies one of the more positive forms of silence: the silence that makes space for dialogue. An implicit agreement on shared goals allows for groups with different agendas, working on different issues, to come together. They focus on their commonalities rather than their differences. Thus, one silences one's individual voice in favor of a common goal. Otherness recedes into the background in the interest of achieving social change. In the African-American struggle for racial equality, this concept has its roots in the nineteenth century with founders like Frederick Douglass and Harriet Tubman. During the Black Power period, Huey Newton referred to this concept as inter-communalism. Like Randolph and most of the unionized Black laborers, its adherents were mainly Black socialists.

> Following the release of Newton in June 1970, Panther leadership abruptly shifted its politics from internationalism to inter-communalism. Newton philosophically contended that socialism doesn't exist because "nations have been transformed into communities of the world."[1] This fourth stage in Panther evolution in part impelled Newton to shrewdly take sole leadership of the BPP and consolidate its operations in Black Oakland, in the attempt to integrate and control the community at a mass level in preparation for the last historical material stage, Communism – a utopian community like Democracy with political ends to be strived for, but which had yet to be historically achieved.

> The cornerstone principles of inter-communalism were dialectical materialism and power. Dialectical materialism was an intellectual tool based on the constant synthesis of forces in opposition to one another that Panther members used believing that "it increase[d] [their] ability to deal with [the] world and shape its development and change." Power interrelated within this intellectual construct was the ability to exercise agency and "control the phenomenon around [oneself] and make it act in some desired manner."

> Politically, the Panthers were philosophically more inclusive and reformist under inter-communalism. Under Newton, the BPP intellectually found relevance in movements, institutions, and activities that they previously shunned, such as the Peace Movement, the Women Liberation and Gay

Movements, Black Capitalism, the Black Church, and participating in electoral politics.[13]

At this point, the BPP were moving in the direction of intersectionality. The concept of intersectionality is a new variant and application of the idea of bringing people together to fight discrimination. The term "intersectionality" can be defined as acknowledging "the interconnected nature of social categorizations such as race, class, and gender as they apply to a given individual or group, regarded as creating overlapping and interdependent systems of discrimination or disadvantage. By adding the idea of intersectionality to feminism, [a] movement becomes truly inclusive, and allows women of all races, economic standings, religions, identities, and orientations for their voices to be heard." Prior to the 1970s, social justice groups did not even consider this concept as part of their politics. Adopted from women's and gender studies, the concept of intersectionality is central to the BLM movement. (Indeed, most of the national BLM leaders are educated women.)

While Black Lives Matter may represent an affirmative use of silence, Herb also highlighted two far less positive aspects present today in the struggle for racial equality in America: the silence of hopelessness and the silence of fear. In his opinion, the silence of hopelessness should not be underestimated. After certain advances were made towards equality in the 1940s (with regard to employment), the 1950s (vis-à-vis education) and the 1960s (in relation to housing and accommodations, voting, and affirmative action), since 1970, progress has slowed; in some cases, drastically.

Herb spoke in depth about the bifurcation of Black America. Blackness in America is seriously fragmented today. In this division, two very different types of silence can be discerned. Both are engendered in response to oppression, and each of them serves to further widen the gap between the two groups. The ramifications of such silences run deep.

On the one hand, one can note those who observe silence in order to fit into the mainstream. Throughout the "Baby Boom"/Civil Rights eras, some African Americans were able to take advantage of the opportunities that became available and joined the middle class. These people

---

[13] This explanation was provided as background material from a forthcoming article by Herb Ruffin II (see reference list).

now inhabit predominantly White spaces in terms of work and education. In the drive to become first-class citizens, desire for opportunity and equality has led many in the process of acculturation to either assimilate into the mainstream culture or even give up their original culture; many have become disconnected from their old communities. Such people have often adopted a mainstream way of thinking, culturally disconnected from a traditional or stereotypical racial identification. According to Herb, increasingly, many children of these upwardly mobile African Americans do not even identify as Black. They see themselves as individuals, rather than as members of a particular race. They maintain silence about their heritage.

Herb refers to this as "the ultimate peculiar situation, the act of double consciousness: as an African American who lives as an American without regard to race." Such a person has bought into the myth of color-blindness promulgated in the mainstream media: that American is a multicultural space – which it is, but in a largely segregated way. (Think, for example, of the appropriation of Rap music by suburban White youth, or rock and roll, or jazz.) Some young people have been shocked back towards a more traditional perspective, as the myth of post-racialism has been exposed as a myth, most specifically after the murder of Trayvon Martin and widespread police violence against young Black people across the USA.

In stark contrast to the Black middle class – which is, in itself, not really comparable to the White middle class – there exists what might be called a Black "underclass." Members of this group exemplify the silence of oppression and hopelessness. They are truly disadvantaged and disempowered. They are frequent targets of police violence and state violence. Children in this class "rarely rise above the tracks which exist in public education which too often seem to lead Black youth directly either to prison or the military." Herb refers to this group as

> "post-proletarian," the descendants of working-class Black people who are now disconnected from living wage manufacturing and manual labor employment. Most of these millennials are people who have never seen the hope of upward mobility that came out of the "double victory" movement of the 1940s... For generations, this class has been living in neglect... While things were going great for White America, it was not so for African America... [they have been] the main victims of austerity, of the military and prison industrial complexes... Gangs have become

super-gangs, organized often by local officials, and always under the threat of the new boogeyman: increased drug use and drug trafficking.

Even more depressingly,

> any spaces that could have propelled them into the middle class have disappeared for a large population... the old pathway towards the middle class is now closed. Many African Americans became civil servants in the 1960s and 70s, but due to massive cuts in education and government, that pathway is no longer available. This is the worst situation African America has been in since the 1970s. They also have the largest "middle class" ever in their history.

The structure of American society as a whole reinforces this kind of double consciousness for all races: desegregation and integration often exist in the same physical spaces. Both are organized by mainstream American systems.[14] The city of Syracuse itself, where Herb lives and works, is the ninth most segregated city in America, where ghettos (mainly Black) and affluent suburbs (mainly White) exist side by side.

Another nationwide trend has worked against the development of authentic and widespread equality: the ongoing realignment of the American political economy. Mainstream America has become more and more conservative, resulting in a gradual constriction of social welfare programs, and spending cuts that would have allowed for more affirmative action, fair housing initiatives, and so on. What served African Americans well in the original Civil Rights movement ("a rising tide" effect) is now seen as a threat to economic stability.

The silence of fear has been present throughout the history of Black America. As Herb put it,

---

[14] This institutionalized racism was documented for example in the Kerner Commission report (see reference list). July 1967, US President Lyndon Johnson created the National Advisory Commission on Civil Disorders, headed by Illinois governor Otto Kerner, to explore the background of the urban race riots and to recommend solutions. In signing the order establishing the commission, Johnson said he was seeking answers to three basic questions about the riots: "What happened? Why did it happen? [And] what can be done to prevent it from happening again and again?" Sadly, it would seem that in 2016, a new report is needed.

you may be conditioned to be silent. If you think you are going to be lynched, you may well go quiet on it. But if accommodation politics turns out to be ineffective, you need to become more active, to get change to occur.

Ruffin related one striking example of the silence of fear. In 1968, civil rights activist Anne Moody published a memoir called *Coming of Age in Mississippi*. In it, she recalls hearing of the death of 14-year-old Emmett Till (a boy her own age), who was killed in 1955 "for whistling at a White woman":

> Before Emmett Till's murder, I had known the fear of hunger, hell, and the Devil. But now there was a new fear known to me – the fear of being killed just because I was Black. This was the worst of my fears.

Her own fear did not paralyze Moody. Rather, it galvanized her into rebellion. As she spoke to family members about the event, she realized that "her mother, her grandmother, everyone" knew about what had happened, and about many other Black people who had been treated as Till had been. She found herself becoming increasingly angry at the silence perpetrated by her community, for not protesting against such injustice.

Experiences like these led to a new shift in the behavior of Black Baby Boomers, which eventuated in the Black Power movement.[15] As Baby Boomers have given way to Millennials, expectations have changed. "Gen Y.2" has been raised in the era of "big data" and standardized testing, which focuses on racially imbalanced, market-driven research, rather than on the educational and social needs of children in disadvantaged communities. These trends are not new; but they manifest now in more exaggerated forms than previously. Societal values have changed in line with the commodification of education.

This generation has been raised in the era of the World Wide Web, of instantaneous communication and a demand for instant gratification that often seems to be unaccompanied by reflection on consequences. It is

---

[15] For example, Moody broke with her family to become a member of the nascent civil rights movement, joining the Congress of Racial Equality (CORE) and the NAACP (National Association for the Advancement of Colored People) and spearheading voter registration efforts. She participated in the original Woolworth's lunch counter sit-ins and the 1963 March on Washington.

possible that the escalation of gun violence and road rage over the past 20 years may also betoken similarly unreflective responses to frustration. It is certainly noticeable that concurrent with changes in expectations regarding the speed of accessibility of communication, America has become more violent. For example, gangsta rap paved the way for hyper-violent Chicago "drill music," and for "trap" music, an excessively aggressive form of Southern rap.[16] In addition, video games (like *Grand Theft Auto*) have played a role in the desensitization of young people to violence and the blurring of lines between actual and virtual reality.

Millennials want to see the immediate results of their action. The type of education they receive does not, in general, foster interest in blending disparate ideas or on seeing where ideas intersect; they think more along the lines of a single track. They tend to be more goal-oriented, "how can I get to where I want to go?" This trait first appeared in the generation after the Baby Boomers – the first "ME" generation of the 1970s: Generation X, who first popularized hip hop.

This expectation of accelerated change would appear to hold true even about expectations of activism. Ruffin notes that both the War on Drugs and hip hop music came into being around the same time (1973).

> Hip hop was originally a form of political statement and community entertainment. The 70s was a time of heightened political awareness and engagement. From the 1960s through the mid-70s, people working for social justice exercised direct action: sit-ins, teach-ins. They were interested in bringing about large-scale, systemic change. Much of this was non-violent.

In some ways, activism looks very different today. Often, "old" tactics may still be in play, now facilitated through technology. Often, "their 'gun' – versus the guns being pointed at them – is the cell phone." Rather than occurring through large organizations, today's activism takes place in atomistic, fragmented pockets of social media: "A pocket can really be anyone with a cell phone or a Twitter account." For example, the "Dream Defender" group in Washington DC is run by a handful of people, and the

---

[16] That being said, however, it is important also to note the sensationalization and corporatization of rap music which has, at times, threatened to transform rap into an updated minstrel show, disconnected from the communities and experiences from which it originated.

so-called Black Lives Matter movement is actually a conglomeration of over 300 small groups. They (BLM) are now joining with other small groups like the Oakland Blackout Collective, to focus not just on police violence, but on a broad range of issues.

Intersectionality does not come naturally to this generation, but may be a necessary corrective to the movement. Herb observes that:

> Instead of coming from a place of unity, today, all [the activists are] coming from very different directions. This is not new: it happened during the New Negro, Civil Rights, and Black Power movements. What is new is that they don't follow the rules of respectability politics; they are out there doing their thing in their own way. Wanna-be leaders have to demonstrate that they know what they are doing: Millennials will ask you *why* something needs to be done, that is how they are being raised.

As with the original Civil Rights movement, much of the activism today employs a mixture of strategic silences and direct action. The bifurcation of Black America means that there is a renewed distinction between respectability politics and "irrespectable" base politics. Again, this feature in itself is not new; the first break with respectability politics occurred during the Black Power period. Now, the distinction between the two types of action is more extreme. The first type is largely middle class:

> The Arab Spring/African Awakening – all are, for the most part, middle class movements. The face of the movements are people who may not look middle class, but actually are – Trayvon Martin, for example.

The second group – which is more inclined to direct action, to putting their bodies in harm's way – is less interested in respectability, and "they don't look as respectable as the people at the lunch counter." This aspect of the movement is closer to the Black Panther philosophy of social change: "if you can't do it legitimately, you have to do it 'by any means necessary': by empowerment politics. Yet often, even this aspect of the movement has a largely non-violent intention. Rather, what is violent is their mere presence; which, sadly, is often perceived by police and 'the state' as threatening."

Herb has been writing about and observing the history of African Americans for nearly 20 years. In the summer of 2015, Herb had an experience in which the political became intensely personal. In the USA in 2015, over 100 unarmed Black men were killed by police. Thirty-seven percent of unarmed people killed by police in 2015 were Black. Overall in 2015, Black people were killed at twice the rate of White, Hispanic, and Native Americans.

In July 2015, Herb returned to Claremont, California, for the first time since completing his doctorate. As he went from the home of one former professor to visit a friend, he was accosted by eight armed police officers, "three–four police vehicles with at least seven Glocks and shotguns ready to murder." Without preamble or explanation, the officer in charge

> harshly ordered me to put my hands up. He did not ask for my information. My [Black] colleague...who was also questioned over who owned his home, informed the police who we were – as if professional credentials should matter when deciding who should be treated as a first-class citizen in a democratic nation.

This outrageous – and potentially deadly – situation was quickly defused, but

> for over 15 minutes [the police]...tried to justify their actions by telling me that crime rates were up in Claremont, particularly along the border (Towne Avenue) which separated rich, predominantly White Claremont from working class Pomona; also that my appearance and actions "fit the profile" of people who were robbing homes, "who were mainly African American men."[17]

For many years prior to this event, Herb had already been a board member of BlackPast.org (an online reference guide dedicated to African-American history) and of several other national academic organizations in his field. He has been involved with student groups working on racial and social justice since 1993: as an undergraduate, then as a graduate student, and, since 2008, as a faculty member. As someone who grew up in and with the hip-hop movement, Herb feels that he can move between the two worlds of the old and the new. He is "aware of the stark divides [between them],

---

[17] This account is part of an op-ed piece written by Herb, which no mainstream news outlet accepted for publication. He eventually published the piece on a blog, and it has been submitted for publication in an academic journal (see References).

and this is what [he brings] to the table." The experience in Claremont accentuated the personal nature of his political stance.

In addition to his ongoing research, his own activism takes two main forms, "within institutional lines, trying to protect students from being too exposed," and, even more quietly, working for curricular reform "under the radar," especially in those areas of the American West where the racial atmosphere is often "very conservative and sometimes downright hostile." ("One legislator in Arizona called 'ethnic studies' equal to communism.") Herb has family in Texas who teach in the public education system. He worked with a cousin to create an introductory African-American studies course for a high school curriculum. He notes this as a means of surreptitiously helping change to happen. "Even in hostile places, you can accomplish something."

All seven of the modalities of silence that are shaping our discussion appear within the one cycle of silence explored in this interview. The fivefold process implicit in each of the modalities of silence is also embedded in the case. When we began these analyses, we wondered if and in what manner all the elements of the fivefold process would emerge in each case. As our work has progressed, we have several realizations.

First, as we mentioned in the previous chapter, the fivefold process of attending to silence is not linear. Rather, it is intertwined with and integral to events. While it is important to observe when the various moments of the process arise, it is equally important to take note of the interpretation people give to the events over time. That is, what does silence mean to the individuals in their specific context?

In every case, silence is conditioned by a number of factors. We need to observe not only the individuals alone, but also their interactions with the groups they belong to and the groups they want to belong to. That's why experiencing the act of attention is so vital: someone has to actively pay attention to the various silences in order to look at their meaning. Otherwise, it is unlikely that forward movement will ensue.

Furthermore, silence is not abstract: it has both concrete manifestations and recognizable implications. It is also not without its prejudices. As we have seen in this chapter, silence is often strategic. This may or may not always accord with the global good. It is important to remember that there is always a value bias attached to silence.

Examining and interpreting this bias has helped us to understand something else about the dynamic nature of the fivefold process. Our initial hypothesis was that the fivefold process might be a complete cycle within each case. However, this is not always – or necessarily – the case. But even when the cycles are not complete, they are nonetheless rich; they continue to break open into new possibilities/modalities.

In fact, the fivefold process is not so much cyclical in nature as helical. As far as the theory is concerned, it is not a double helix like DNA, but actually a multiple helix. The process is not a matter of neat or complete beginnings or endings. One can witness many combinations of modalities at any one moment – like the inscription of silence into one's own thinking, which may occur at several different times. Neither all the modalities need to be completed, nor the fivefold process in its entirety. There will be some people who do not complete the analysis of silence through full engagement, but start to react before undertaking a full analysis. Or, on occasion change may occur not (or not only) as a conscious act of reflection on silence, but rather (or also) based on an unconscious prompting by the historical/cultural particulars of a specific context.

REFERENCES

Carroll, Joseph. "Public Overestimates UPS and Hispanic Population". http://www.gallbuup.com/poll/4435/public-overestimates-us-black-hispanic-populations.aspx.

Federal Bureau of Prisons. "Inmate Ethnicity." https://www.bop.gov/about/statistics/statistics_inmate_ethnicity.jsp. Accessed June 9, 2016.

Gold, Alex, Edward Rodrigue, and Richard V. Reeves. "Why Are Black Americans at Greater Risk of Being Poor?" *News Week Magazine* (August 2015) http://www.newsweek.com/why-are-black-americans-greater-risk-being-poor-361543.

Journal of Blacks in Higher Education. "More Than 4.5 Million African Americans Now Hold a Four-Year College Degree." http://www.jbhe.com/news_views/64_degrees.html. Accessed June 10, 2016.

Kerner Commission. http://www.politico.com/story/2016/02/kerner-commission-report-released-feb-29-1968-219797#ixzz4N0erUDFE.

Knauss, Tim. "Report: Syracuse and Onondaga County Suffer from 'Hyper-Segregation'." *Syracuse News* (November 2014). http://www.syracuse.com/news/index.ssf/2014/11/report_syracuse_and_onondaga_county_suffer_from_hyper-segregation.html.

Moody, Anne. 1992. *Coming of Age in Mississippi: The Classic Autobiography of Growing Up Poor and Black in the Rural South.* New York: Dell.

Reeves, Richard V. and Edward Rodrigue. *Brookings* Institute *Social Mobility Memos.* (January 15, 2015). http://www.brookings.edu/blogs/social-mobility-memos/posts/2015/01/15-mlk-Black-opportunity-reeves.

Ruffin II, Hebert G. 2011. "A. Phillip Randolph". In Matthew Whitaker. (Ed). *Icons of Black America*, Westport, CT: Greenwood Press, 727–739.

Ruffin II, Hebert G. 2015. "Which Came First, Jim or James Crow?: De Jure Racial Discrimination Revisited". In Sherwood Thompson. (Ed). *The Encyclopedia of Diversity and Social Justice*, Lanham, MD: Rowman & Littlefield Publishers, 448–452.

Ruffin II, Hebert G. "Black Lives Matter: The Growth of a New Social Justice Movement." Blackpast.org. http://www.blackpast.org/perspectives/black-lives-matter-growth-new-social-justice-movement.

Ruffin II, Hebert G. Winter 2015. "'Doing the Right Thing for the Sake of Doing the Right Thing': The Revolt of the Black Athlete and the Modern Student-Athlete Movement, 1956-2014." *The Western Journal of Black Studies*, 38(4): 260–278.

Ruffin II, Hebert G. 2017. (Forthcoming) "Struggle on Multiple Planes: California's Long Civil Rights Movement." In Bruce Glasrud, and Cary Wintz (et al.), *The Modern Civil Rights Movement in the American West*, Norman, OK: Oklahoma University Press, ca.

Shapiro, Thomas. 2004. *The Hidden Cost of Being African American: How Wealth Perpetuates Inequality*. NY: Oxford University Press.

United States Department of Labor, Bureau of Statistics. "Economic News Release." http://www.bls.gov/news.release/empsit.t02.htm. Accessed June 9, 2016.

University of California Berkeley, Office of the Chief Financial Officer, Office Planning and Analysis. http://opa.berkeley.edu/uc-berkeley/fall/enrollment/data/2015.

White, Gillian B. "How Black Middle-Class Kids Become Poor Adults." *The Atlantic Monthly*, January 2015. http://www.theatlantic.com/business/archive/2015/01/how-Black-middle-class-kids-become-Black-lower-class-adults/384613/.

CHAPTER 9

Visible Silence (Poland/Germany)

Respondent Background
Ela Wysakowka Walters
Ela Wysakowka Walters graduated in 2011 from the University of Fine Arts in Posnan, Poland, with a degree in intermedia arts. Her choice of that designation was intentional and significant. She is a proponent of the artist Dick Higgins, an American member of the Fluxus movement (1958–1978). Higgins (1938–1998) invented the term "intermedia" to describe a rising trend of artists working across the boundaries of traditional media, or integrating recognized "fine arts" with new, sometimes experimental methods. Higgins held the conviction that the task of a modern artist was "to connect the dots, rather than disconnect the dots and follow just one path." Thus, while Ela sometimes works with traditional media such as paint or chalk, she also learned how to blend and integrate non-traditional media. In that way, she is an example of interdisciplinarity.

> I am a visual artist but I could also study and train in inter-media – that's very important to me. In that way I could choose from everything that the university has to offer, both traditional media and modern media, and I could find teachers who are interested in trending media – things not necessarily usually classified as fine arts.

Words are also very important to Ela. Prior to training as an artist, she obtained a degree in English. Her initial goal was to become an English teacher, but she has instead "naturally followed the path of the translator." In this way, she explains

> I am able to "marry" two paths, because most of my work is translating texts about philosophy and art. It's a rather narrow specialization, but marries two paths. This is my main source of support. Being an artist is insecure job in any country. Translation is the source of funding for my art projects.

Ela feels that the two paths complement one another well. Most of her translation projects are for academic journals, so the majority of the work is fairly dry and technical. But she feels that this type of tedium is actually quite helpful to her process as an artist.

> If I didn't have that practical skill, I think I would go the path of the poet [she was referring to the American poet Wallace Stevens, who worked for his entire life as a clerk in an insurance company]. Because creative work is so demanding, you get woken up in the middle of the night, sweating, with an idea. It's very draining. A boring job gives you a rest, otherwise your brain overheats.

In fact, Ela's artistic work "marries" the two paths equally well: the core of her art is the translation of silence. Translation is a creative activity. So is understanding silence. A translator occupies a liminal position: between an original text and its translation, between what already exists and what is merely potential. In relation to meaning, a translator stands in the open space between what has been said and what is about to be heard and understood, or between what has already been thought and what is about to be thought in a new medium. In and from that liminal space, a translator creates new opportunities for understanding.

Silence, too, can represent that sort of opportunity. Ela's artistic work discloses a way in which the creative process and the element of silence can be mutually beneficial to the task of improving our ethical decision-making – as we shall see.

Historical and Cultural Context

The focus of our interview was on an installation that Ela had constructed in 2011, in a town which no longer exists: Kupferberg. It was established in the fourteenth century and, as its name suggests, was a center of copper mining. At its peak, the town had 160 mining excavations, but the industry died out in the sixteenth century. In the mid-nineteenth century, the town strove to reinvent itself, and became a popular tourist destination, known for "its picturesque location, splendid beauty and a wonderful climate."[1]

Like many towns in the region, after the restructuring of German borders in 1945, Kupferberg was placed under Polish administration and renamed Miedzianka.[2] As happened throughout the region, The Potsdam Agreement effectively introduced a sort of ethnic cleansing of the town: all of the native Germans were transported to Germany and replaced with Poles.

While these population shifts were happening above ground, however, a different operation was going on underground in Miedzianka. There the Russian military was secretly carrying out uranium mining. From the 1940s to 1950s, 600 metric tons of uranium were sent from Miedzianka to the USSR, but officially, Miedzianka housed a paper factory. Everything was done with the utmost secrecy; some Polish miners were even executed in order to keep the mining secret.

---

[1] http://rudawyjanowickie.pl/en/villages-in-the-rudawy-janowickie/436-miedzianka.htm

[2] At a conference in Potsdam in 1945, the Allies agreed that the harsh reparations which had been imposed on Germany after World War I had so seriously affected the German economy in the 1920s that they had contributed to the rise of National Socialism. In order to avoid repeating that error after World War II, the Allies resolved to provide assistance to help Germany rebuild its economic and social infrastructure. They recognized that it would take a considerable length of time to reconstitute a truly democratic German national government. Therefore, under the Potsdam Agreement, four countries (the USA, Britain, France, and the Soviet Union) were designated to run a disarmed and demilitarized Germany in four zones of occupation. The Potsdam Agreement also called for drastic revision of the pre-war German-Soviet-Polish borders, and the expulsion of several million Germans from the disputed territories. Poland both lost and gained territory in this process. It ceded land to the Soviet Union, but received a large area of German territory as compensation. Poland then began to deport the German residents of that region (as did other states with significant populations of German residents).

The exploitation of the town was performed in a rather haphazard manner. No plans were made beforehand to reinforce the structure of the town that had been built over the mineshafts. It is not surprising, therefore, that in the late 1950s, some of the houses started to collapse. But it wasn't until the 1960s that an official, planned destruction of Miedzianka started. First, bans on repairs were issued, and then demolition began. The inhabitants of the town were moved to the nearby city of Jelenia Góra, and the town was effectively abandoned.

In 2011, a group of PhD students (and their professor) from the University of Fine Arts in Posnan were invited by local authorities to tackle the difficult topic of Miedzianka. Former residents of the town and local historians wanted to memorialize the town in some way. They were given a book which had been published earlier that year. *History of a Disappearance: The Story of a Forgotten Polish Town* was a collection of individuals' eyewitness accounts. The team set off to spend a week doing research in the abandoned town. Ela recounts:

> When I arrived there, I was struck by an [overwhelming] feeling of suspension. Everything was suspended: people, time, place. I spent my time reading the book... walking around the place, and trying to imagine what [it] used to look like. It was very difficult, as the "town" is now basically a forest. [There are] no street markings or any other markings which would guide the imagination as to what the town used to look like. I decided to focus on the feeling of suspension.

She soon discovered in the book a fragment that detailed the demolition of the Protestant church.

> The account was very dramatic. It talked about huge amount of explosives – such a massive amount that when they were detonated, the entire church lifted up in the air as a whole. According to onlookers, for a moment the whole church hung suspended in the air before dissolving into ash. The last thing that landed on the ground was a sphere. I realized that I would like to do something absurd: I would like to hang a sphere right where the church had stood, [at the same spot in which it would have been if it were still attached to the structure of the church].[3]

---

[3] Such spheres are a common element in German church architecture; they are frequently found at the base of the weathervane. Ela used old postcards of the church to recreate the original sphere. It measures 40 centimeters, and it is levitating about 15 meters above the ground.

As the interview progressed, it will become clear how this installation is an illustration of visible silence, and how crucial the process of exploring silence is to Ela's artistic work.

Case Analysis

Of the seven modalities of silence, Ela felt that the two which pertain most organically to her are attentive listening and the silence that makes space for dialogue. These modalities are deeply entwined in her artistic work; one might almost say that they are essential elements of both the process itself and her own creative goals.

Ela's perspective on attentive listening is closely aligned with the theme of anxiety that we raised in the opening chapter. She feels that

> in fine arts, silence is a tool that you have to learn, the same as learning how to use a brush or pencil. From day one, you have to learn the opportunities that silence brings, and how to use it. The way you use silence in your work is as unique to you as a fingerprint, just as how you use a brush is unique to you like a fingerprint. Every artist has a unique way of using silence. It's a part of learning to concentrate.

As with any other tool or technique, the use of silence is not "second nature" at the beginning. Rather, it requires careful and methodical training. Once one has "mastered" the use of silence, it becomes just another implement with which to make art.

> It's so much part of my creative process, I can't think of any time when [I had a problem with silence]. I mean, when I was young, there were probably times when I was talking too much, but nowadays it is such an important part of me that it's impossible for me to think that it could be threatening... It's almost as if one asked me "do you have a problem with a pencil?" How can you have a problem with a pencil, a pencil is just a tool that I am using – it's the same with silence.

Ela resonated immediately with the fivefold process.[4] "I could basically sign my name to that – it looks very much like the workshop that I created last year." As part of her doctoral course, she had to perform some

---

[4] See Chapter 2, pages 12 ff.

teaching duties. She decided to design an experimental module. This consisted of 15 90-minute class meetings. The module focused on three topics: brain function in the creation of art; creative blocks; and silence. The workshop presented an interdisciplinary approach to using silence in art-making. One of the sessions was dedicated to analyzing working methods. For her, thinking about silence means considering simultaneously a number of levels of creativity:

- The creative process itself and its various elements
- The systems within which one is working (e.g., is the piece a commission? an assignment? a response to an internal impulse or an external stimulus?)
- Neurobiology (what is happening in the brain while the creative process is taking place)
- The practical aspects of using silence as a tool
- The idea of questioning. This last point applies to the work as a whole: Why does one create? How does creativity happen? Where does it come from?

This last set of questions is reminiscent of Martin Heidegger's famous essay "The Origin of the Work of Art," where he, as a non-artist, raises some of these same questions, from within his philosophical/phenomenological framework.

Just as one does not simply pick up a brush and begin to paint, one does not plunge into silence. First, one has to prepare the tools, the environment, and the artist. Creativity begins long before pen is applied to paper, or paint to canvas. Neither does it end when the object is ready for display. Rather, creativity is a continuous process which develops and evolves over time. As one moves through the process, both explicit and latent forms of silence emerge. These interconnected forms of silence serve as conduits of creativity. The first step is to cultivate an active interior silence, making space inside oneself for the work to develop.

> If you are going to begin work on a very hard or complicated project, warm your brain up first. Look through your notes, design alternative models of your project, talk it over with someone, be active.

Ela encouraged her students to begin by cleaning their workspace; switching off their phones and all other media; choosing a time when email and other social media will be checked; and finally, practicing mindfulness: entering into the present moment with one's mind as clear as possible of distractions. She feels that it is important, at that stage, to immerse oneself in silence; in fact, to plan for one to three days of silence. During that time, she recommends always carrying a notebook, and maintaining silence as much as possible, even while enjoying physical work, exercise, running, and so on.

Then, one can begin the process of reflective inquiry. The first question is not about what medium or design will be employed. Rather, it is a meta-question; it takes a step back from thinking about how the artifact will be produced. Instead, the process begins by inquiring into why: "When have you created anything just for the joy of creation?" She then asked the students to define their topic as well and as fully as they could, to gain a sense of the aim of the piece, what they wish to communicate through it, the audience they wish to reach, and so on.

If and when a blockage occurs, Ela suggests "switching off" from the topic for a while:

> Do something completely different, relax. Your limbic system will carry on working for you in the background. You rest. Consistently break your mind's strategies: look at things from different perspectives, go for a walk, or do something else.

The process of "switching off" is also a form of silence, through which one can enter into another aspect of the creative process. The process itself thus entails the creation of spaces.

Ela encourages artists to enter into the kind of judgment-free state that we have referred to in earlier chapters; taking a pause from conscious reflection to allow the mind to continue processing on a pre-conscious level, using its technical acumen and experience, but keeping the ego at bay as much as possible. She explains that this is necessary because of the anxiety that silence creates.

> When you start your training as an artist, first of all there is a fear of silence: it's intimidating. You have to understand that, and not back away from it. You have to tame the silence, and understand it is working to your benefit, not against you. There is an element of anxiety about the silence that you have to accept as part of the process.

She feels that the anxiety is a natural and necessary part of the creative process, the process of bringing something new into being.

> Anxiety comes from the way our brain works, the way we are used to living. Our brain optimizes everything, it works according to schemata, to patterns, like being on automatic pilot: we know what to expect, [we know] that everything will fit into a pattern. Anxiety appears when a non-standard solution begins to appear.

For Ela, silence is an organic and inescapable part of the creative process, and both the silence and the act of creating provoke some anxiety.

> A creative idea is something unique appearing, so some silence is part of the creative emergence. The brain wants to have an easy, familiar shortcut. Silence informs us that there is a different solution, a *new* solution about which we don't yet have information, something is going to reveal itself to you; it's a tricky situation [for the brain].

Ela maintains that "becoming friendly with silence, inviting silence into the work" opens the space into which creativity can appear. This practice – like any other artistic technique – must be learned carefully and intentionally.

> It has to be a part of your training: to become an artist, you have to learn that those moments of silence and anxiety are your friends, because this is the threshold. You cannot create without the silence, you have to go into the silence, through attentive listening. It's only in that silence that you begin to hear the connections that you cannot predict, where the new ideas are emerging.

The idea of using or managing silence is not new in the teaching of art, but

> until now, in art education, it was indirect. The teachers didn't really speak about silence as part of your formation. It was there, but you had to work it out for yourself, and then you could talk to the teachers about it. Now that is changing. Now, with developments in neuroscience, people are talking more about silence in the process of creation, and it's a topic people would like to investigate, right along with the other tools and artistic techniques.

Ela has also found the topic being discussed at conferences about art pedagogy.

At one conference I attended a presentation by a professor from the Faculty of Design at the Academy of Fine Arts in Warsaw. Her entire course is about silence. The students cannot use words in any of their assignments. They are given five questions to solve over the course of the semester. They can only use the bodies, the contexts, the environments that they encounter; their answers cannot use any words whatsoever. So we saw people squeezing into tight spaces, or trying to be as motionless as possible. Where it's not being deliberately spoken of, silence is definitely coming up to the surface.[5]

Here we begin to reach a new level of understanding of one of the guiding questions of our initial research: how can silence be recognized and revalued as a means of improving ethical interactions, as a tool for social transformation? Perhaps Ela's example can begin to point us in that direction. Human nature is such that in general, people are only able to consider changing their behavior if they feel safe in doing so. If people feel threatened in a situation, they tend to retreat into familiar ways of acting and interacting. At the very least, they tend to "take a stand": anxiety provokes and promotes a certain rigidity which might be mistaken for strength. However, if anxiety is lessened, there may be more flexibility, a greater willingness to consider compromise.

Perhaps, then, one avenue towards meaningful and positive social change is to help people to manage their anxiety, and one means towards that goal is to help them to reach the kind of "threshold point" that Ela mentions here. This idea can be expressed in a number of different ways. One might ask: does the creation of silence require one to reach a threshold point before we can learn to manage our anxiety about what we are confronting within our zone of effect? Or one might say: one way to reach that threshold point is through the intentional creation of silence. Thus, creating silence is necessary because it helps us to reach that liminal standpoint (as we suggested in Chapter 1) from which we might be able to consider a new approach. Once people realize the importance of the threshold, they might be motivated to find ways to seek it more actively.

One of the reasons that silence is so valuable in this endeavor is that it helps us to connect seemingly unrelated aspects of our knowledge base. Here again, Ela provides a helpful illustration. As homework, she asked

---

[5] It would be fascinating to chart the rise of interest in silence overagainst the rise of background noise in contemporary society, but that question will have to wait for another opportunity.

her students to go through the following process of thinking and questioning at the outset of a creative project. The first step is to choose a topic that they will then try to express visually: for example: "silence without silence." Here is the assignment:

> Please go step by step through the following tasks:
>
> a) Look for opposites: Re-word the topic, so that it means the opposite
> b) If you are to deal with the concept of "silence without silence", then try to answer the following question: What could silence co-occur with?
> c) Suggest something that not everyone does (in the context of your topic)
> d) Consider unlikely pairings, using the question: "What if?" Use the following opposites: stretch/ shrink; freeze/melt (For example, related to the concept of "silence without silence": "what if the world were frozen into silence, what force could cause it to melt?"
> e) If silence can be said to exist even "without silence", is it possible to strip it of anything else? If so, what? What would that *look* like?
> f) Ask yourself the "WHY?" question five times. Write down the questions and the answers. [This is a means of getting deeper into the question of why you have chosen this topic, and why it matters.]
> g) Ask pragmatic questions:
>
> - *What* do you mean by "silence without silence"?
> - *Where* have or might you encounter this phenomenon?
> - *When*, under what circumstances might this occur? How might it come about? What might be its origin, what might bring it to an end?
> - *Why* would this be a desirable or undesirable condition?
> - *Who* might be affected by such a state of affairs?
>
> h) Next: Imagine the following processes happening to or within or around the topic that you have in mind:
>
> - What would it look like if it increased/decreased?
> - How might it change?
> - What other conditions might it be linked to?
> - How might it be used (and by whom)?
> - How might it move from one place to another?
>
> i) Stop
> j) Rest
> k) Stay in silence for one to three days, keep your notebook close.

What Ela is doing with this exercise is taking the students through an analysis of silence. This is not achieved by reflecting on a particular silence. Rather, she encourages them to pursue actively the question of how to communicate with the silence we observe. Thus she inquires more deeply into the heart of the idea: Is "silence without silence" possible? What does that phrase mean? Here we need to be careful not to fall into the trap of dualism: thinking about binary opposites like silence/non-silence, or equating silence with passivity and non-silence with activity. It might be helpful to bear in mind that silence is not empty, but rather full (of potentiality). The phrase "silence without silence" invites us to look beyond the binary, beyond dualism, to a possible new way forward.

However stimulating the choice of example may have been to Ela's students, it was certainly thought-provoking for us, as silence researchers. From our perspective, "silence without silence" is a rich and dynamic silence. It is the silence of active and attentive listening: actively using one's understanding, actively searching for meaning, while trying to keep value judgments and preconceptions to a minimum, in order to keep the way clear for something new to emerge, for the creation of a new solution.

The reflective quality of the silence that we understand as the modality of attentive listening is a way of being silent in order to understand where we are, to get our bearings. In previous chapters, we have remarked that on occasion, silence – like the silence of fear or oppression – begets more silence: the *kathoey* is silent in the face of intimidation because she is afraid of repercussions; this silence may then be co-opted as assent. Or the child of "disappeared" Argentinians, now in adulthood, may silently question the past, but maintain silence into the next generation. In the previous cases, people reacted to the silence of or in their circumstances with more silence. They entered, so to speak, into a tunnel of silence.

The silence of attentive listening has a different trajectory. Rather than simply perpetuating more silence, this modality engenders new methods of understanding and making use of silence. One of the ways in which we manage silence is by finding hidden connections – the sorts of correlative links that Ela's questions are meant to draw out.

One can make an analogy here to the Miedzianka sphere. From a distance, it seems to be floating in mid-air: one cannot see the wires on which it is suspended. Similarly, the silence of attentive listening can connect seemingly unrelated concepts and hold them in our attention.

A comprehensive analysis of the process of creation, then, can become a new way of managing silence.

The goal of the installation was to bring together disparate elements: to draw attention to the contrast between what was currently in that space and what was no longer there.

> That was my first aim. The second was to communicate how I felt about the place: *I* felt suspended. I realized that I needed to communicate the emotion that the place gave me, of being between two places. It's a kind of "No Man's Land", like [that which] exists between borders. The site is there (you can google it), but it's not there. No one takes ownership of it. It does not leave the past, and it's not really moving to the future. That place [itself] is silence.

The installation that she created holds the dynamic tension of the silence of the in-between space. It presents the quality of attentive listening in a visual format.

The second modality of silence which Ela found relevant to her work is the silence that makes space for dialogue. For her, this modality is more complicated than the first. Ela distinguished two separate phases of the "life" of a work of art: the creation of the piece and what happens to it after its creation. She began with the second:

> When you go to a gallery, even if the artwork has an audio component (an audio or video tape), it remains silent, because the creator is absent. The object is positioned in a gallery, but it's left there by the creator. That situation in and of itself creates space for dialogue. You have the object and the viewer who comes to experience it, and the dialogue is happening between the artwork and the viewer. This is the most important goal.

From her perspective, just as silence is an integral part of the process of fashioning the work of art, it is also an integral part of the piece over the entire span of its existence. The distance produced by the absence of the creator creates a silent space in which the work of art and the viewer can interact. Marcel Duchamp (1949) said that a work of art was completed not by the artist (whom he refers to as a "medium"), but by the viewer:

> Let us consider two important factors, the two poles of the creation of art: the artist on one hand, and on the other the spectator who later becomes the

posterity; to all appearances the artist acts like a mediumistic being who, from the labyrinth beyond time and space, seeks his way out to a clearing.

This term "clearing" (*Lichtung*, in German) is central to the philosopher Martin Heidegger's understanding of how "the fullness of what exists" (i.e., material and non-material reality, *das Sein*) reveals itself through the individual phenomena of the world (*das Seiende*) to beings who are conscious of being in a specific time, place and condition (*Dasein*). More simply: the clearing is where we catch a glimpse of the way things are, in the context of existence itself. This liminal or in-between space is, for Heidegger, a space where truth can become manifest.

It is important to remember that the truth that is emerging is a truth that is steeped in silence, and that silence is not the same as stillness or stasis. Silence is always teeming with potentiality.[6] It is dynamic, always in motion. By the same token, the threshold or "clearing" is not merely an empty space waiting to filled in order to reduce our anxiety. If we can step away from the binary paradigm, we find that the silence may in fact be full: replete with the ebb and flow of existence. The silence need no longer be limited or fixed to the in-between space. In some important ways, the in-between spaces disappear – or at least do not have solid boundaries. They become more permeable, and they seem to be floating, rather than fixed. What emerges into the in-between spaces are the connections of new ideas. The threshold does not separate two closed sets; rather, it is a hinge point between multiple worlds of possibility. As we suggested in the opening chapter, silence contributes to ethical action in part because it permits one – or perhaps obliges one – to pause at the threshold of a decision.

For Ela, the silence of the artist's absence becomes an invitation to dialogue; and is an essential part of the creative process.

> That is *exactly* what a good artist is supposed to learn; this is *precisely* the process that you have to learn as an artist, in order to be able to create good art – because an artwork is an invitation to the other, a contribution. If an artwork is a closed-off question, there is no life in it.

---

[6] The dynamic nature of this silence finds an analogue in quantum field theory. In the quantum vacuum, no physical particles are present. But the vacuum is by no means empty: it is full of fluctuating electromagnetic fields. This state is sometimes referred to as a "zero-point field."

> My teacher Leszek Knaflewski told us a story. It was a warning. If you create a work of art, and people come to see it and say "Aha!", then you have failed. If they come and they think, "That's stupid, what is that??" If it makes them *think*, that is a success. Your job is to make people carry the artwork with them in their minds when they leave the gallery.

The people who leave "carrying the artwork with them in their minds" are performing acts of visible silence as well. They are transcending time and space by bringing what they have seen out of the space of the gallery into their own contexts, pulling the absent artist into their time and space.[7]

As we noted earlier, the creative process does not stop with the artist. Silence is the node of connectivity between the ebbs and flows of existence, between the moments of the spiral or helical movement. The silence can connect people: artists to viewers; those absent to those present; and perhaps it can also connect those who have different viewpoints or objectives that initially seem unbridgeable.

The first aspect of "the silence that creates space for dialogue" connects back to the artistic process itself. This aspect of silence is much more straightforward:

> Once you have gone through the process of learning what your silence is all about, you become proficient at it. You use the type of silence that works best for you, just as you use the brush stroke that is most effective for you. And you understand that your silence is inevitably leading to the dialogue. Just like the story about the "aha" – when you are making the artwork, you have to incorporate aspects of silence into the artwork in order to make space for dialogue. It's very technical and deliberate.

For Ela, the installation in Miedzianka exemplified this facet of the work of silence.

> I went to the place and spent many hours researching it, trying to feel it, to understand its silence. Whilst there, I went through the stages of field research. Field research in the arts is different from what is usual in the social sciences. In arts, field research involves the fivefold process as well as intuition, conversation, and gathering data (visual, oral, written). This technique is not as well researched as social science techniques, but it is

---

[7] We shall return to the notion of "active presencing" in the final chapter.

very clear and precise. When I went there, I was analyzing the silence, analyzing the facts of the place, the topography, and then drafting plans.

Then I had to take a decision: what would be the optimal artwork to communicate this feeling with the minimal amount of expression? Then, when I finished, I just left it there, with no inscription, no information about it, no signpost about the past history of the place. I just left a sphere hanging in the forest, and the sphere is [gradually] ascending to heaven, because the trees to which it is attached are growing.

The work of art awaits the viewer in silence. As the trees continue to grow, the sphere moves higher. The silence and the state of suspension are unbroken. They are active and vibrant, open-ended. They are still communicating. The dialogue continues.

And here is a funny thing about it: when I went back there two years later, I discovered that people have adopted it. Mountain guides have now incorporated into their tours of the area. The sphere becomes an excuse to talk about the city that is no longer there. That was not my intention – so this is really a dialogue [that people have taken in a new direction]. My intention was simply to show the absurdity of the whole situation: it is as absurd that the sphere is there as that there is a forest growing on top of a city that is no longer there.

The dynamic encounter with silence can shake people out of their habitual modes of thinking. Confronted with the silent sphere, some viewers may become conscious of their anxiety about the silence. They can then take the opportunity to manage that silence. At that point, it enters history again. It becomes a point of connection, and of dialogue: they began to talk about it in an effort to create meaning.

This interview reinforced the significance of the dynamic nature of silence and how it impacts on the process of creation over time and space. Integral, continuous, dynamic over space and time.

References

Duchamp, Marcel. 1949. "The Creative Act". Paper presented at *The Western Round Table on Modern Art* [Transcript of Proceedings], ed. Douglas MacAgy. San Francisco: San Francisco Art Association. In *The Writings of* Marcel *Duchamp*, Michel Sanouillet and Elmer Peterson. (Eds). New York: Da Capo, 1973.

Heidegger, Martin. 1977. "The Origin of the Work of Art". In Trans. William Lovitt. *The Question Concerning Technology and Other Essays*, New York: Harper Torchbooks.
Higgins, Dick. 1987. *Fluxus: 25 Years/November 7, 1987 - January 3, 1988*. Williamstown, Massachusetts: Williams College Museum of Art.
Milonni, Peter. 1993. *The Quantum Vacuum: An Introduction to Quantum Electrodynamics* 1st *Edition*. New York: Academic Press.
Springer, Filip. 2017. *History of a Disappearance: The Story of a Forgotten Polish Town*. Trans. Sean Bye. New York: Simon and Schuster. (Originally published in Polish in Czarne, 2011).

CHAPTER 10

The Healing Qualities of Silence (Uganda)

> **Respondent Background**
> **Samite Mulondo**
> Samite Mulondo describes himself as a musician, a humanitarian, and a man of peace. He began to play the Western flute at the age of 12 and quickly became one of East Africa's most acclaimed flautists, with a promising concert career. In addition to the Western flute, Samite now plays a number of African flutes and other traditional instruments, like the marimba (xylophone), kalimba and mbira (thumb pianos), litungo (harp), and drums.
> Samite fled Uganda in 1982 at the age of 25. Several members of his family had already been killed, either by soldiers loyal to Idi Amin, or by rogue "bandits" who capitalized on the atmosphere of terror promoted by Amin's regime (see below). After a couple of very close brushes with death, Samite decided to leave Uganda as a political refugee. After five months in a refugee camp, and a total of five years as a refugee in Kenya, Samite made his way to the USA.
> Since that time, he has made his living as a professional musician, spending several months a year on tour. Not only is he a performer of world music, he is also a performer on the world stage. Samite has worked in the studio with Paul Simon and Will Ackerman, among others. He has toured with Ladysmith Black Mambazo, Windham

Hill, and a host of other world-class musicians. He has produced ten solo CDs for international release and composed the soundtracks for (and appeared in) a number of documentaries. Two of these are about Africa and were released on PBS. *Song of the Refugee* (1998) is a documentary about Samite and his return to Africa after being away for ten years. *Taking Root: The Vision of Wangari Maathai* (2009) is the biography of the Nobel Peace Prize Winner. His other movie score was for the national award-winning films: *Addiction Incorporated* (2012), about the scientist who blew the whistle on "Big Tobacco" in the 1980s. Samite and his music are featured in *Alive Inside* (2014), which explores the power of music to reach patients suffering from Alzheimer's disease and other forms of dementia.

For two decades, Samite has devoted himself and his music to the promotion of peace. In 2002, he founded "Musicians for World Harmony,"

> an organization dedicated to enabling musicians throughout the world to share their music to promote peace, understanding, and harmony among people. In that capacity he travels to sing, play music, and exchange stories with victims of war, poverty and HIV/AIDS. He has traveled extensively in the war-torn and distressed countries of Uganda, Kenya, Congo, Rwanda, Tanzania, Latvia, Liberia and Cote d'Ivoire to work in refugee camps, with former child soldiers and AIDS orphans.[1]

He is frequently invited to these facilities by UNICEF or other NGOs, and by private individuals working with different groups.

When we interviewed Samite, he was on his way to spend two weeks in Uganda working with children affected by "nodding syndrome," a neurological disorder of uncertain etiology. Some medical authorities believe that it is caused by toxic chemicals in the water, which may have been poisoned by rebel fighters as they withdrew from the border region between South Sudan and Uganda. Alongside a music

---

[1] http://samite.com/bio.

therapist, Samite uses the local music of the children and their caregivers as tools for healing.

Throughout his professional career spanning more than three decades, Samite has performed at a variety of events that promote world peace. These include performing for the Dalai Lama in Ithaca, NY, and, at the 2009 *Vancouver Peace Summit: Nobel Laureates in Dialogue*, hosted by the Dalai Lama Center for Peace and Education. Additionally, in the fall of 2011, Samite performed and spoke at the UNHCR 60th Anniversary Celebration in New York City.

HISTORICAL AND CULTURAL CONTEXT

Little documented history is available about Uganda before the seventeenth century. By the time records began to be kept, power was shared between five tribal kingdoms. The Buganda kingdom became the most powerful by the nineteenth century, having developed a strong standing army and a well-developed agricultural economy. This kingdom was ruled by *"kabakas"* (traditional kings), who were advised by a council of chieftains.

Kabaka Mutesa I invited English Protestant and French Catholic missionaries into the country in the mid-nineteenth century. The sympathies of the people eventually divided into three parties: some loyal to England, some to France, and some to Islam (having been influenced by trade coming through Sudan). The country became a British protectorate in 1894.

Over the first half of the twentieth century, the economy of the country flourished through its production of cotton, sugar and coffee. Indigenous legislative and executive councils were established in 1921, and by 1955, the country had begun to develop a party-political system. Uganda became fully independent in 1962. Its first constitution gave federal status and semi-autonomy to four of the five traditional kingdoms, of which Buganda was the most powerful. The *kabaka* of Buganda (Kabaka Mutesa II) was appointed as the ceremonial president (head of state).

This situation lasted only a very short time. The Uganda People's Congress, led by Milton Obote, was backed by people from the northern half of the country, but relations were tense with the formidable southern kingdom of Buganda. Four years after taking office, Obote revoked the constitution of 1962. The following year, the kingdoms were abolished, and Obote became both the president and the prime minister of Uganda in 1967.

Obote ruled the country mainly as a police state for the next four years, intimidating and terrorizing his political rivals. In 1971, however, he himself was ousted through a military coup staged by one of his former officers, General Idi Amin. Obote fled just over the border to Tanzania with the remnants of his army.

Amin also proved to be a ruthless authoritarian. Within two years of taking power, he had expelled all Asians from Uganda (Asians had formed the majority of the trading middle class) and seized their property. He also confiscated the property of the Jewish community and waged an internal war on anything he deemed "intellectual." His regime quickly degenerated into violence and mayhem: murder, looting, and rape became commonplace. These actions had a devastating effect on the country's economy and society. It is estimated that during the eight years of Amin's regime, between 100,000 and 300,000 Ugandans were murdered. In 1978 Amin declared himself "President-for-life" and invaded Tanzania. Obote's army of exiles joined forces with the army of the United Republic of Tanzania, and soon succeeded in re-taking the capital, Kampala. Amin escaped and fled the country for Saudi Arabia, where he lived until his death in 2003.

After a tumultuous two years, Obote was again returned to power in 1980. Sadly, his return to power did not mean the return of peace for the country. Obote's second term in office was marked by economic and political instability and continued violence. One faction (the National Resistance Army [NRA], led by Yoweri Museveni) never accepted the results of the 1980 elections and carried on a guerrilla war against Obote's government.

In 1985 Obote was ousted by another military coup, this time led by General Tito Lutwa Okello. Okello did not receive the approval of the NRA either, and after just a few months, his government was overthrown, and Museveni became president in January 1986. Museveni inherited a country in which civil war had cost the country a million deaths, two million refugees, more than 500,000 seriously wounded citizens, and the utter devastation of its economic, political, and physical infrastructure.

A decentralized parliamentary system was set up over the next few years. From 1989 to 1996, slow progress continued towards economic and political stability. Although civil war continued in the north of Uganda for the next three years, Museveni's administration was more democratic than the previous military dictatorships of Obote and Amin. Museveni put in place a non-party political structure, in an attempt to avoid the ethnic divisions which had plagued the nation for so long. In practice, however, this became a one-party system.

In 1996, Museveni was elected president with 75 percent of the vote, and a national assembly consisting of 276 individual members was formed under what was termed the "movement system." The constitution of the new state required that a referendum be held on this system in 2000. An overwhelming majority (91 percent of a voter turnout of 47 percent) voted for the system to be maintained. Museveni was elected for a second five-year term as president.

Conflict between Museveni and previous colleagues in the National Resistance Movement continued for the next few years. During this time, Museveni's government was also engaged in a perpetual power struggle with a rebel group led by Joseph Kony, the so-called Lord's Resistance Army (LRA). Eventually, in 2006, a ceasefire was effected between the Ugandan government and the LRA. The ceasefire led to a truce, then peace talks facilitated by the Government of South Sudan. This fragile truce was maintained until June 2007, when the Ugandan government finally reached an agreement with the LRA on a plan for long-term peace, reconciliation, and accountability.

At the time of writing (2016), Museveni has been in power for 20 years. Since 2000, incremental progress has been made towards the development of a multi-party system and the rebuilding of the country's economy. However, serious questions remain concerning the validity of elections, the involvement of Uganda in conflicts in the Democratic Republic of Congo and Somalia, and South Sudan, and the true nature of democracy and human rights in Uganda, especially with regard to freedom of speech, gay rights, and the rights of women.

Case Analysis

For Samite, silence does not signify a lack of communication. On the contrary, he sees silence as an essential feature of communication. In his work, he manages silence in order to enhance communication and promote healing and peace. Throughout his life, Samite has experienced most of the fivefold process and the modalities of silence on an unconscious level.[2] He sees his work of healing as a methodology of silence, of the attentive listening to which we referred in our opening chapter.

> Listening is the most important thing that we are missing. If you are loud, you can't even hear what the other person is saying. It's all about listening.

For Samite, silence is integrally linked with both hope and hopelessness. Whether he is working with refugees, former child soldiers, or people with dementia, he often finds that silence expresses a lack of hope. In a noisy and violent world, it is often hard to hear hope. Unconsciously, Samite has realized that one way to deal with hopelessness is to be comfortable with silence, and to use silence to help open a channel to healing, by giving people hope. So long as one has hope, the power of silence can enable one to transcend a hopeless context. Even if the hope is illusory, an imaginary construct can provide enough hope to motivate someone to begin to participate in a healing process.

Samite has also observed significant differences between voluntary and involuntary silence. Being forced into silence is different from electing to be silent. If one has embraced silence voluntarily, one is able to move from one modality to another: from the silences of hopelessness, oppression, and fear into the silence of attentive listening or the silence that make space for dialogue. If one has been forced into silence, it is difficult to feel a sense of agency about silence: it becomes a symbol of oppression. Thus, it is not seen as a property to be managed, and the silenced person does not see himself as having the agency to manage it.[3] To be able to move between processes – let alone to transcend one's circumstances – requires hope.

Samite recounted several very different influences on his understanding of silence: from childhood, his adolescence, his time in the refugee camp, and his humanitarian work. His maternal grandfather was a major influence in the development of his character and on his relationship to silence.

---

[2] See above, chapter 2, especially page 12.

[3] This "voluntary" silence is reminiscent of the "Musselmänner" of the Nazi concentration camps. In *Remnants of Auschwitz*, Giorgio Agamben refers to those who had become so physically weak and emotionally shut-down that they no longer even spoke – nor were they spoken to – even by their fellow inmates. Their silence was an eloquent expression of their utter dehumanization.

Samite remembers him as "different from everyone else." His grandfather was a member of the Bugandan elite: very wealthy, and related to the *kabaka* (tribal king). Most unusually for his culture, because he was not at all interested in material possessions, he turned over all his "miles and miles of" land to his wife. Samite recalls:

> He wore wooden shoes – he could have afforded leather shoes handmade in London, but he chose to wear these wooden shoes. If he saw that I was making a big deal of a thing that I was given (a flute, whatever), he would say: "Then again..." And I was supposed to finish the sentence: "...they are all material things to be left behind."

"Leaving things behind" can also be interpreted as a form of silence: a voluntary withdrawal from acquisitiveness. A deeply spiritual man, his grandfather would use his machete to create clearings in the forest as meditation spaces. This action too illustrates a form of voluntary silence: consciously connecting to nature, to what is important in life. Samite recalls:

> Often, I would be sent to get him. He would not answer me; he would not respond until he was ready. That meant I had to wait and meditate too.

A second major influence stems from growing up under Idi Amin's brutal regime. In this example, the silence of oppression and of fear can take a voluntary turn, in which one chooses not to give up, but rather to connect to others in a different way.

> Another way to be silent, the way we survived in Uganda in Idi Amin's time, was not to confront anybody. Not to engage at their level. Some did that: some joined in with the violence. I chose the way my grandfather would have done it – to be quiet and "come in" a different way. My brother [who was later killed by Amin's soldiers] joined the forces. I come back at people... by giving them a voice. I help them to remember there is happiness, through the healing power of music. This is a different way, as compared to picking up arms and blowing up bridges.

Samite told two anecdotes from his adolescence which explicitly connect silence and death. On one occasion, he and some young friends stole out to go to a dance. After the dance, they encountered a roadblock as Samite drove them home. In the dark, they could not determine whether this was an official roadblock or an ad hoc one set up by bandits. As they got close, they realized that it was unofficial, and that they were in imminent danger of being kidnapped or worse. As they sped through the barrier, the "soldiers" opened fire on the car. Samite did not stop until he had put a safe distance between themselves and the roadblock. At that point,

> I said to them, "It's ok, you can get up now [from the floor of the car]. Is everybody ok?" One by one, I called their names: "Stephen, you ok?" "Yes, I'm here." "Richard?" "Yes." "Hope?" After a long moment of silence, Hope answered. Finally he said, "I'm ok." He was badly shaken, but unharmed. It turned out that a bullet had come within two inches of his head.

Samite recounted another anecdote from his pre-refugee days. As he got older, he continued to perform, steadily gaining a following in Kampala. On one occasion, he noticed two policemen silently following him. He stopped to have his shoes shined and consider his options. The man shining his shoes noticed the policemen too. He simply said, "I'm sorry, man." Too often, when the police singled you out, arrest and murder would swiftly follow. Samite decided that when they came for him, he would not go quietly.

> I had been studying martial arts since I was 12. So I thought, "When they come to grab me, I'll hit them with everything I know. At least I will die fighting." After what seemed a very long time, they came up and said to me, "Samite, is that you?" I said, "Yes," but I didn't turn around. I planned how I would attack them by surprise without turning. Then one of them said, "Samite, don't you remember us? We were on traffic detail at your last concert. We love your music!"

Samite realized that if he didn't leave the country soon, he would go the same way as his brother had gone: into violence. He escaped to a refugee camp over the border a few weeks later.

One of the few sources of entertainment in the camp was a single television screen on which the same four episodes of the American program *Dallas* were recycled. The guards would frequently turn off the screen at random moments and order the inmates to return to their dorms. At that point, two types of silence became evident: the silence of insolence and the silence of oppression. Perhaps surprisingly, the people who demonstrated these modalities were not necessarily those whom one might expect. In the camp, one was silent about one's past. Thus, all shared a silence of relativity and equality.

> I [had been] brought up in a wealthy atmosphere: everyone had a Mercedes, "things" were very important. In the camp, life changed. Everyone was the same: doctors, rich people, lawyers. It took me back to my grandfather's values.

In the camp, the ordinary balance of power was inverted. This inversion gave rise to new silences. For example, those who had had power underwent an involuntary silencing. And those who had previously been silenced developed a voice. The guards were quiet, but not silent.

> The guards only spoke when they wanted to order us to go somewhere. Those guards, in their class – poor, not educated – would ordinarily not be able to speak to those people – the wealthy people. But now there had been a power shift. [The guards] were angry, but they couldn't express it... they used negative energy to push others down: "I'm going to put you where you've had me for so long." It's loud in their head, but they don't know how to [articulate] it.

For their part, the inmates were also silently angry.

> There was a lot of anger. The people would think, "Who is he to do that, to turn it off when I was enjoying it and order us back to the dorms?" But it wasn't safe to say anything.

All of this silent anger could have been quite explosive had it not found an outlet in the form of the "king" of the camp, a former street beggar named Sanday. He had had polio as a child. He couldn't walk, so he hadn't gone to school. Illiterate, and a talented pickpocket, he found a way to defuse the anger.

> Sanday was the king of the camp because he could transport us out of the camp with his stories. He gave us freedom to get out of the camp with his stories. [Listening to] Sanday would take away the anger. [It] would make us quiet and silent, feeling light.

Samite feels strongly that the world's problems are rooted in the principles and practices of inequality.

> I think the first thing we have to do is get rid of classes. We have to respect all people equally. When it came time for me [to emigrate], I didn't want to leave the camp. I felt for the first time what it was like when everyone was respected equally This was interesting for me: how we all wanted to sit around the "king's bed": this street beggar.

The experiences he had in the camp changed Samite profoundly: even more than the experiences of violence in or displacement from his homeland.

> It changed the way I looked at life. I was a different man. Now, since then, I talk to anyone. Sanday opened my eyes. He even made me think back, "This is the way my grandfather used to look at life."

Samite sees himself as following in Sanday's footsteps, but with one vital modification: he consciously incorporates an element of silence into his work.

> [Sanday] didn't open up a space for others to tell stories, but I do something different: I create a situation... a space for people to talk, to tell their stories. Whoever it is: a child soldier, a senior in a nursing home, I leave them room to tell their story. I don't take over the whole time. My grandfather used to listen to people like that, he didn't interrupt... and he treated everyone the same, no matter who they were.

For Samite, the silent space allows for a connection to emerge. He has seen this happen many times, in different contexts; to him, it is a key component of his work.

> Why do I leave the space? Because we all have stories to tell... when we let others tell their stories, it helps them in their healing process, and for the hearers, it helps us too. For example, I was performing at an orphanage in Kenya. There was one girl, she was about 15. I noticed that she didn't participate through the whole thing; she didn't clap or anything, she was just watching from the corner. At the end, when I was leaving, I was packing up my instruments. She came over to me and said *"That's* what you do for a living? That's *ALL?* Have you gone through *ANYTHING* difficult in your

life?" She was judging me – she thought I was from a different class, and that I have not suffered at all.

The young woman perceived difference as an unbridgeable distance between them. She could not feel any connection to Samite; thus, his music could not touch her. How could healing occur? Samite needed to break through her judgment so that she could open to what he had to offer her.

So I said to her, "Yes, I have. Two days after Christmas, my wife couldn't pronounce my name. She tried to say my name, and all that came out was 'Sss...Sss...Sss...' So I took her to the hospital and they found she had a brain tumor the size of a golf ball...and then she died."

At that point, the young girl changed completely. She started rubbing my shoulders, and she said, "The pain is not going to last forever. It will go away. My mum was pregnant. She was almost ready to have the baby, but then she got malaria. It went to her brain, and she took a knife and stabbed herself, trying to cut the baby out. They both died right in front of me. The pain was awful. At first I thought it would never end, but over time it gets further away." Telling that story was healing for her. She wanted me to heal too, she wanted to comfort me.

The girl was able to step out of her isolation and pain into the space of silence, and so begin to be with another in his pain. In Samite's mind, the silence is crucial to the process.

Communication definitely requires you to create a space: if we all created spaces and all listened – there would be better communication.

Samite recounted another occasion on which silence created an opening for healing. While on tour in the USA, he had asked his agent to book him into a place where patients were receiving chemotherapy. This was in Cedar Rapids, Michigan, where in 2015 the population was 92 percent white.

I saw this one guy who was getting chemo. I could tell by the way he looked at me that he was not used to seeing black people. I asked him, "Can I play for you?" He just shrugged. I noticed that while I was playing the flute to him, his face softened. When I stopped, he said, "What the hell is that thing around your neck?" He was interested in me. So I told him a story about the Wodaabe tribe in Africa where the men wear makeup and compete for the attention of the women. He opened his eyes wide and said "I'll be damned, tell me more." Then he looked at the port on his arm [where the chemo was going in] and said, "I hope this works. I don't think my wife can handle the farm, the tractors are so big..." When his wife arrived, he yelled out to her, "Hey, come and meet Samite, my new best friend!" [Like the girl in the Kenyan orphanage,] he was judging me. He's probably only seen a black man being put into a police car. But then he saw that we can laugh together, that we both have fear, we both have pain. The only reason we were able to do that is because we listened to each other.

Samite deliberately introduces silence into his storytelling and music performance in order to create the spaces required for this deep communication and communion. He finds that others are not the only ones judging: he too often has to remind himself not to judge.

I do my best to suspend judgement. Sometimes I have to really work on it. If you walk in a room of 70 child soldiers, you know, they're rowdy, they smell like teenage boys. My eyes go to their fingers, and I think, "What have they done with those hands?" I have come up with ways of not going there... I'll play something on a little wooden flute which takes me and them into a very calm place, and then I forget about judgement. When they sense that shift, when they sense that you are not judging them, then they feel comfortable sharing their story with you. Sometimes they want to hear *your* story. The communication begins with not judging, just listening, being ready to talk if asked. It begins when I consciously make an effort to calm myself and them. Because first comes judgement, then comes fear – and they can sense that.

Developing the skills needed to use silence in this way has taken Samite many years. Paradoxically for a musician, his appreciation of silence has deepened over this time.

The first time was in Rwanda and Liberia. I didn't know I could get people to talk – I didn't know you could open people up with a flute, just playing a little something, and then they would say "I have a song, too" or a story. Sometimes the kids will say: "I'm going to make new friends; all my old friends died."

As his humanitarian work has developed, he has found that fear, hopelessness, and oppression have continued to increase. Thus, his work is more important than ever.

> Kony and his people have taken it to a new level. They've learned to exist only on negative energy driving them, for years. How? I don't know.[4]

He tries to suspend judgment even of the most violent factions, such as members of the Lord's Resistance Army, who have carried out brutalities against innocent civilians for the past 30 years. Samite says he would welcome the opportunity to try to show them a different way.

> If I was given a chance, if they wouldn't kill me, I would probably play them a little thing that would bring out their soft side, bring them to tears, get them to leave the "macho" behind.

If he could do that, Samite feels that he could communicate even with these hardened guerrilla fighters. If his safety could be guaranteed, he would welcome the opportunity.

Samite has converted his private tragedies into a personal mission. At the end of the day, Samite said, all he can do is go on in the way his grandfather showed him: respecting all people equally, listening to them carefully, and creating spaces into which he can invite them to join him on a path towards peace:

> It's the only thing I know how to do: to give people hope.

References

Axe, David and Tim Hamilton. 2013. *Army of God: Joseph Kony's War in Central Africa*. New York: Public Affairs.

---

[4] Joseph Kony is a Ugandan warlord who since 1986 has led the LRA. Originally established in protest against the regime of President Yoweri, the LRA is responsible for much of the continuing conflict in central Africa. Kony instructs the members of his LRA to abduct, threaten, destroy, mutilate and murder civilians. He kidnapped over 30,000 children over 30 years, forcing the boys to become soldiers and the girls to become sex slaves for his officers. See: http://invisiblechildren.com/conflict/kony/.

Dagne, Ted. 2010. *Uganda: Current Conditions and the Crisis in North Uganda.* Columbus, Ohio: Bibliogov Publishing.

Jerry, Sampson. 2016. *Uganda History, Historical Legacies and Social Divisions, Uganda before 1899: Idi Amin Rule, Early Political Systems, Government, Ethnic Diversity.* Self-published on CreateSpace.

Mulondo, Samite. Web page: www.samite.com.

Mutibwa, Phares. 1992. *Uganda Since Independence: A Story of Unfulfilled Hopes.* Trenton, New Jersey: Africa World Press.

CHAPTER 11

Reflections

Our Original Intent and Hypotheses

We began this project with an intuition that silence is an important ethical component of communication. With each interview, our initial hypotheses were confirmed and strengthened. We gave our respondents very little background information before an interview; we simply told them that we were studying how silence manifests itself in different cultural contexts. We were often amazed at how aptly their responses to our questions matched and then extended our original understanding. As we conclude this part of our research, we would like to suggest some strategies which we hope may contribute to improving and enhancing ethical communication and decision-making.

Our primary goal in undertaking this research was to examine the role of silence in the process of decision-making. In the opening chapter, we introduced the idea that decisions begin well before any action is taken. The conscious mind is always already aware of both itself and its surroundings, and taking into account the effects and consequences of actions on past, present and future relationships. This is simply a part of the phenomenology of mind. Our aim was to explore how a specific type of mindfulness might drive the decision-making process.

From the outset, we felt that attention is an essential element of silence, that reflection is equally key, and that ethical communication requires a fundamental attitude of openness to and respect for the other. What we did not expect was how much more we would learn along the way. We did not realize, for example, how many layers of silence could be revealed in one situation, and how similar issues, questions, and attitudes about silence would arise over and over again with comparable urgency and salience. In each case, several distinct silences co-existed in one conversation, and each carried with it far-reaching implications for decisions. It was clear from our reflections that on many occasions, silences were more significant than the spoken discourse. At the same time, we did not appreciate that variances in cultural norms and constructs would prove to be far less significant than the universal qualities of silence which we observed during the course of this project. We were also surprised to find that interpretation of silence often begins with the one who is generating the silence, not the one who is on the receiving end of some silent communication. In this final chapter, we take a look at what we have learned, and suggest some ways in which our research can be applied.

Four central questions guided our research. In each case, we had first to consider how silence was present in the situation at both micro- and macro-levels (i.e., looking at the person in the context of his or her community). Next, we inquired into the way silence emerged and is understood. The answers to those questions informed our analysis of the implications of each of the modalities of silence which we identified. Finally, we sought to discern how various aspects of silence could be reimagined to promote positive social change in an ethical manner.

Our exploration has given us many new insights into the nature of silence. The topic has often been studied from the standpoint of involuntary silence: exploring the experience of those whose voices have been ignored or suppressed; whose silence is a reaction to trauma, aggression, or oppression; or where silence seems the only possible response to what is unspeakable. Our process has attempted to maintain a balance between those types of silence and silences which are actively chosen for a variety of reasons. Our interviews seem to indicate that voluntary (and sometime even involuntary) silence can be generative. Rather than problematizing silence, we feel that it is possible to understand silence as an important resource which might be used to increase awareness, promote unity (either within a group or between disparate groups), and construct new paradigms of thought and dialogue. These are just a few of the ways in which silence can be used to improve the quality of decision-making processes.

In the course of our research, we uncovered several aspects of silence which we had not previously appreciated. For instance, in Micronesia and Northern Australia, we found that silence was more structural than functional. Culture often promulgates a systemic mode of behavior including what, who, and when individuals may talk and/or be silent. Where this occurs, silence is woven into the very fabric of a society. Thus, significant ramifications appear, for example between insiders and outsiders (represented by the etic and emic perspectives). Therefore, at times it was nearly impossible to extricate the individual's experience of silence from her cultural context.

In Southeast Asia, Guyana, and Poland, our original epistemological framework – the seven modalities, the fivefold process – appeared to have been already embedded within each respondent's ontological context. Of course we tried not to superimpose our hypotheses onto the data. Rather, the interviews revealed that the silences were created by the events in which our respondents found themselves, and to which they sought an ethical response. We made a conscious attempt as researchers to silence our own preconceptions and judgments in order to avoid drawing premature conclusions and foreclosing new thoughts that might emerge from the data. By employing this method, we strove to embed an open, attentive, and reflective silence into the very research process itself.

The way in which one understands silence is markedly different depending on whether one is operating from a primarily emic or a primarily etic point of view. If silence is perceived as reflecting the internal logic of a particular culture, it is difficult to see how movement is ever possible – either for an outsider to move into the meaning-structure of a group's self-understanding, or for an insider to move outwards, to create new meaning. Relying too heavily on an etic perspective (based on pre-established theories and conceptual constructs) can hinder one's ability to respond to silence in an open and generative manner. On the other hand, the etic perspective may offer the capacity to observe and reflect on one's situation in a way that enriches both self-awareness and inter-subjective attentiveness.

Both the etic and the emic perspectives build upon the foundation of reflective self-consciousness and self-determination. Our research shows that effective management and use of silence seems to be integrally linked with the emergence of the self. Dealing consciously with silence in one's life has striking parallels with the process of becoming an individual through reflective self-awareness and self-determination. In both cases, a decision has to be made with regard to one's fundamental attitude toward the other. This attitude begins with attention, which can lead one to observation, analysis, and definition: of the issue at hand, of the other, and of oneself in relation to the other. Self-consciousness is both a goal and a result of the act of attention. Through attending to, responding to, and redefining an issue, new aspects of self-understanding may develop.

Silence has a particular role to play in this process precisely because in some ways silence transcends language, subjectivity, and rationality. As we have suggested in various chapters, silence sometimes occupies and sometimes creates a liminal space; for example, between subjects, between conscious and unconscious reflection, between rationality and imagination. The dynamic nature of silence can provide opportunities for attention to break through internal barriers (constructed by the ego) and external barriers (constructed by society).

In the silence of attention, we hold open the doors of possibility. This is not so much an action as a state of being, a condition. Attention can inhabit a pre-reflective space, in which the distinction between self and other is still more fluid than fixed. Because it occurs in a neutral and (more or less) free space, it is a positive and hopeful point of departure. Self-consciousness emerges from attention, as awareness (simultaneously) of differentiation and responsibility. Such a practice may require us to move beyond dualistic thinking. Perhaps we need to learn how to "drift alertly" into hitherto unfamiliar spaces.

Product and Process: Moving Beyond Binaries

The reflective and interdisciplinary nature of our project means that we do not think of this final chapter as a conclusion, but rather as an opportunity for the beginning of a new level of inquiry. It would be antithetical to the nature of our work to present our "findings" in this chapter. Rather, we simply hope that we have laid the ground for future conversations. Our methodology was based on our understanding of what we have called "strong interdisciplinarity": an attitude that we were not constructing a project that could be finalized, but rather were – and are – engaged in a dynamic and open-ended process.

In large part, the research question itself gave rise to the methodology. The ethics of silence requires us to search for what undergirds attention as a process and not as a product. For us, the purpose of communication – silent and expressed – is not only to reach a decision or to link actions over time and space. Ethical silence is reflective and reflexive: an ethical attitude to silence requires one to reflect on oneself, the other, and the silence itself. If that is done, then the process can open up new possibilities and potentialities. Thus, in the course of our interviews, when we observed that a specific theme was emerging, we endeavored to define the elements of the process and the modalities involved, to see what possibilities and potentialities might develop.

In most of the interviews, our respondents began with a shared preconception: that in many interactions, silence is overlooked because it is not considered a significant aspect of communication. Frequently, silence is considered to be a consequence of an individual's past experiences. This assumption may be accompanied by a fear of the unknown: what might happen if one paid attention to silence?

Paying attention to silence has two prerequisites, by our analysis. The first is the development of a conscious awareness that silence exists in every encounter. The second is to cultivate the recognition of that idea in the process of "drifting alertly" into the intersubjective spaces. These translate into the words of Pope John Paul II as similar to the moment of a birth of a person where consciousness and self-determination coexist with each other. The birth of a person through consciousness and self-determination is very similar to the birth of an idea and how one consciously deals with silence in one's life.

What Have We Learned?

The methodology we used to understand the ethics of silence was to pay close attention to what people had to say about silence and then reflect consciously on our conversations. We learnt that there are a number of aspects we needed to attend to beyond the fivefold process and the modalities we considered in the early chapters of this book. The following emerged as some common threads.

Respect: For Elders, for Tradition, for Indigenous Ways, for Self-knowledge Versus "Expert" Knowledge Each interview placed a marked emphasis on the need for silent, respectful listening to the other's self-knowledge. This was especially noticeable in the chapters on Cambodia, Guyana, and Northern Australia. Despite the differences of culture and of social context (i.e., despite the different social roles or functions which the listener might hold), the encounter always called for a fundamental attitude of deep respect. Jarrett said:

> People are the experts of their own realities; we respect them as that. We are not the experts on their lives: *they* are.

Vivian, Jasmine, and Julian each echoed this statement in almost exactly the same words.[1] As researchers, we held it as an essential part of our own process to approach the interviewees with the same attitude, not merely of respect for them as persons, but with an openness to being taught by the encounter. This is a profoundly ethical stance with which to begin any interaction. How different the world would be if every interaction began with a recognition that we should listen attentively to what the other has to teach us.

Silence, Time, and Place Jasmine, Cristina, and Herb uncovered for us the need to increase our awareness of the place and time in which silences occur, and how spatial and temporal contexts impact the manifestation of silence. Cristina, her colleague, and her students were all profoundly moved by particular times and places of silence. Through the fivefold process of reflection, Jasmine became more aware of the silences imposed by her culture, and the effects that these silences had had on her own development and on the development of her people. She also became more aware of the significance of silence in certain times and places. Herb, on the other hand, took note of recurrent patterns of silence over time in the history of the African-American struggle for racial equality.

Silence and Identity Formation In virtually each case, silence played a substantial role in the development of identity: as a way of engendering a sense of self or as a means of self-empowerment. For Cristina, the encounter with silence as an adult brought about a new understanding of the relationship she had had with silence since early childhood – and inspired her to a new attitude toward her vocation. For Jarrett, exploring the struggles for independence from a patriarchal system – first in the context of a church, and then in the context of gender identity – deepened and expanded his own self-understanding and acceptance. Vivian, Julian, Jasmine, Herb, and Samite discovered new facets of their professional selves through their engagements with the silence of others. Ela uses silence to extend the art through which she interprets the world. As researchers, we too have been changed by the process of continual reflection on silence: its meanings; its possibilities; the tremendous significance of what remains unsaid in every encounter.

---

[1] Of course, this is not a new insight for social scientists. However, we felt it noteworthy as an aspect of silence.

Silence, Hope, and Healing The relationship of silence to hope and healing was most readily apparent in the cases of Cristina, Jarrett, and Samite. For all three – whose histories and trajectories could not be more disparate – appreciation of silence has facilitated profound personal and professional growth, and the healing of deep, lifelong wounds. At the beginning of our interview with Samite, he said that "there is only one form of silence." After reflecting with us on his experience of silence, however, he realized that he had unconsciously enacted the fivefold process in his own life. Silence is now so genuinely inscribed onto his experience that even without intending to do so, he now uses silence as part of the healing work to which he has dedicated his life. Moving forward, our hope is that reflection on the fivefold process may serve as a catalyst for similar healing in others.

Silence as an Existential Attitude In the course of each interview, we realized that we needed to think about our fundamental stance toward the person to whom we were listening. On the one hand, we had what might be considered brief and superficial encounters: one-hour interviews, conducted over Skype, consisting of scripted questions following a structured format. In only one case were all three interlocutors physically present together. Most of the time, Ram was in Australia and Nancy in the USA, with our interviewee in a third location. Yet the depth and richness of the content far exceeded our expectations. Each interview offered a glimpse into what the poet Rilke once called the "infinite interior space"[2] of each human person. It also disclosed a potential approach toward being-in-the-world. This perspective contains the idea that the more we listen to an other, the more that other points us toward the mystery of the human experience: what Vivian referred to as "the silence of the unknown and the unknowable."[3] This aspect of silence – the attitude of existential openness to not-knowing – has been central to our methodology.

Silence as Self-Sacrifice Several of the interviews drew our attention to the role silence sometimes plays in putting the needs of the group at the forefront of an encounter and giving a secondary place to the needs or desires of an individual. As we have seen, the reasons behind this use of

---

[2] See, for example, the poem "Es winkt zu Fühlung fast aus allen Dingen" (1914), where he says: "One space extends through all beings: an infinite interior space."

[3] See above, 51.

silence vary. At certain times, the silence derives from a respect for particular persons or sub-groups, or for tradition. On other occasions, silence expresses a discernment that more information needs to be gathered before a decision can be made. In still other instances, silence represents recognition that the time or situation is not yet optimal for a decision. Whatever the reason, silence acts to draw attention to the sense of urgency that often accompanies a poor decision and encourages further reflection. A striking example of this aspect of silence appears in Samite's interview. His grandfather, who acted as such a powerful influence on Samite, would often refuse to answer his grandson until he had finished his meditation. Thus, Samite said, "I had to wait and meditate too." That early model taught Samite his first lessons in silence. It could be argued that without those lessons, Samite would not have survived the subsequent traumas of his life so successfully. Through learning to manage silence, Samite learned how to connect with people, and to connect people, across trauma, loss and fear.

Silence as a Bridge Across Difference   In addition to the functions that it may have within a group, silence also becomes an important part of communication between members of a particular group and outsiders. The issues involved in understanding and responding to an individual who does not belong to one's group are often quite different from those which arise within a group, and must be approached and managed accordingly.

In very different ways, each case (especially those of Vivian, Jasmine, and Ela) raises a crucial question about the management of silence: what role(s) can silence play in encouraging people to think differently about the process of decision-making? Time and again, the interviews introduced the importance of silence in bringing people together who had different types of knowledge. This feature has been especially significant to us in our endeavor to formulate an interdisciplinary methodology. Many times, in the course of an interview, it was observed that perception of difference or distance created the impression of an unbridgeable gap. By careful attention to and management of silence, people were able to reach into and across the spaces in between them. They could reach out beyond their ordinary zone of influence or comfort. The silence created a safe, permeable, and neutral perimeter in which each party could approach the other without undue anxiety: what we have referred to as the threshold.

The Significance of the Threshold   The threshold presents a way to manage contact with others. Often, silence in negotiations is perceived as a breakdown of communication. In our research, we found that the contrary

WHAT HAVE WE LEARNED? 169

was the case. We saw that the encounter with silence frequently provides the means for a breakthrough in communication that facilitates change and engagement. As Ela eloquently outlines in her interview, a confrontation with anxiety at the threshold can serve as a creative stimulus. Overcoming anxiety can lead to the development of new understandings: of oneself or the other, or both. Since we are concerned with decision-making, we have concentrated on the threshold as a potential point of departure.

In fact, this way of thinking about the threshold of silence mirrors findings from neurophysiology about the physical mechanism of hearing.

> Our understanding of how the ear works entered an exciting phase ... when it was discovered that the inner ear actually makes sounds ... [this] discovery was amazing for sensory physiology because it was equivalent to finding that light comes out of the eye (which has never been observed).[4]

Prior to that time, it was thought that listening was a matter of passive reception of sound. In the past 40 years, our understanding of the processes of the inner ear has been revolutionized. It is now known that the inner ear is unique amongst the organs in the human body in several ways. First, its principal cells are surrounded by large fluid-filled spaces. Second, in these spaces, the organ itself produces the chemical fluids which power the activity of the sensory cells. These fluids act like a battery in which electrical energy is converted into mechanical energy. This means that the inner ear acts as both process and product. Third, the outer hair cells of the inner ear – again, uniquely in the cells of the human body – are capable of change in response to stimuli: they can alter their length at acoustic frequencies in response to electrical stimulation. These cells, however, are not only flexible and adaptable, they are also extremely vigorous:

---

[4] Brownell, William. "How the Ear Works: Nature's Solutions for Listening", Volta Review, 1997; 99(5): 9–28. He continues:

"Pressurized cells are common in the plant kingdom but rarely found in cells of the animal kingdom. Plant cells, such as those found at the base of a tree, are highly pressurized. This allows the plant cells to hold the weight of the tree and still be flexible enough to bend and not shatter in a wind ... The analysis of speech appears to take place in parts of the brain that are highly developed only in man. The amazing machinery that accomplishes the reconstruction of the acoustic world relies on the delicate structures of the inner ear that deconstruct the original sounds" (Brownell, op. cit.).

they have to be strong enough to transmit force to the rest of the ear. The fourth feature to be considered here is the membrane that surrounds the pressurized fluid that fills the outer hair cell.

> [T]he outer hair cell is pressurized. Most of the cells in our body will not tolerate internal pressure because the membrane that encloses them has the strength of a soap bubble. A conventional pressurized cell will expand till it bursts. The outer hair cell has reinforced the membrane along the cylindrical part of the cell to prevent it from bursting and to maintain [its] cylindrical shape.[5]

We see a clear affinity between the strength of this membrane and the silence of ethical discourse. Far from being a merely passive/receptive system, the inner ear is the site of intense and multi-layered activity, even before it encounters an external stimulus. In a similar way, the inner subjectivity of each individual is always already the site of dynamic activity even before an encounter with another person. As we move into the final section of this chapter, the significance of this comparison will become clear.

FINAL THOUGHTS, NEW BEGINNINGS

Every voluntary action entails a decision. And every decision (at least if it is to be an ethical one) requires both process and product: a process of judgment, and a product in the form of a decision upon which action can be taken. We feel that it is important to see these two aspects as distinct.

Each decision relies on a judgment regarding past, present, and future: what has gone before, what now presents itself on the agent's horizon, and an imagined future outcome. Taken together, judgments extend the "choice set." That is, they are part of the process of inputs to a decision, elements of the set of variables from which a decision will be made.

At several junctures in our analysis, we have mentioned the idea of "suspending judgment." This is a difficult concept to grasp if we think about judgment as a product; it seems an unlikely or even impossible task. How, for example, can a clinician, an educator, or an NGO worker set

---

[5] Wilfrid Bion, *Attention and Interpretation* (London: Tavistock Press, 1970), 43.

aside his or her knowledge and expertise when addressing an ethical dilemma – and why would she? The problem here is that choice sets can become limited or constrained by fixed theoretical constructs – be they disciplinary or cultural – which block receptivity to the needs of a specific situation. More simply put: how can I hear the other if my head is full of the voice and noise of my preconceptions? If I see the decision in front of me as an "issue," it is already value-laden. If it is a process, then I may be more free to consider other possibilities: to imagine what *might* happen instead of what *must* happen (especially if my judgment has been made along binary lines).

It has become clear to us that in the management of silence, the first step is to become silent ourselves: to cultivate an attitude of interior silence. In so doing, one makes room for something new to emerge. Two helpful strategies toward this end were developed in the early twentieth century, one in philosophy and one in psychoanalytic theory.

The phenomenologist Edmund Husserl (1859–1938) called this process of attention an *epoché*: the intentional "suspension" of cognition for the purpose of studying the experience of the here-and-now. Husserl asserts that the majority of the time, we approach an experience with a variety of preconceptions: memories of past experiences, knowledge about the object at hand, knowledge about ourselves and our usual reactions to people, things and events. Thus, before we engage in an interaction with someone, we have often already decided the shape and meaning of the interaction – thus foreclosing the possibility of learning anything new from the encounter.

Husserl suggested a radical departure from this process. Rather than beginning from the standpoint of what is already known – both about ourselves and about the world – suppose we try to approach each interaction as something *sui generis*, utterly new? He uses the Greek term *epoché* to describe this condition. We suspend – for a moment – everything we know about the world, investigating our experience as original and new.

This shift in perspective allows for the second aspect of Husserl's idea, what is known as "philosophical reduction." Seeing an object, person or event anew helps us to recognize that what we say we "know" is in fact only our subjective apprehension of that thing. That is, it helps us to realize that what we take to be absolute "truths" are in fact merely subjective perceptions. We reduce what we encounter to the parameters of our perception, and then we call that the "truth" of the matter. In fact, Husserl maintains, by moving into and through the *epoché* and the reduction, we are able actually to see the person, object, or event *more fully*, liberated from the limitations of preconceived frameworks, assumptions, and beliefs. We may then see that nothing can be reduced to our perception of it, nor can we be reduced to mere observers or knowers. Rather, the phenomenological process is one of dynamic intersubjective interaction, allowing the other (object, person, or event) to have an effect on us even as we impact upon it. This process of understanding is almost meditative: it calls the knower to be simultaneously present to the experience *and* to transcend it.

How does this process relate to silence? The British psychoanalyst Wilfrid Bion (1897–1979) maintained that "the purest form of listening is to listen without memory or desire."[6] That is, the analyst must set aside any previous ideas about the analysand in order to listen to what is being expressed in the here-and-now. Only then can the analyst really hear what is being said:

> Some silences are nothing, they are 0, zero. But sometimes that silence becomes a pregnant one; it turns into 101 – the preceding and succeeding sounds turn it into a valuable communication, as with rests and pauses in music, holes and gaps in sculpture.[7]

Bion maintains that the analyst should attempt to listen in a silence that requires a suspension of judgment, of fear, anxiety, or aggression – all of which are aspects of the ego. The analyst should suspend reactivity in order to give the analysand the freedom to develop a sustainable gap in which her own individuality can develop.

Without the gaps that exist between subjects, no subject could exist as an individual: we would all share one universal consciousness. Similarly, without the silences that are present in language, communication would be flat, without contours. We propose that the process which we have outlined in this book follows the ideas of Husserl and Bion in this regard.

Bion extended Freud's original framework beyond the mechanistic theory of competing internal drives to encompass both the phenomenological

---

[6] Wilfrid Bion, "Penetrating Silence". Presentation to the Study Center for Organizational Leadership and Authority, Los Angeles, California, December 14, 1976. (Published in *The Complete Works of W. R. Bion, Volume 15* (London: Karnac Books), 31–44.

[7] James Grotstein, *A Beam of Intense Darkness* (London: Karnac Books), 37.

world of others and an ineffable third term. Bion's thinking was not dualistic in nature. Rather, his theoretical structure included "the internal (the unconscious) and external worlds (Consciousness), and the Unknown, which is beyond us externally *and* internally."[8] Because of these insights Bion is widely regarded as having "...introduced *intersubjectivity* (the indivisibility of the two-person relationship) into...general analytic thinking."[9]

Like his contemporaries Rilke and Heidegger, Bion took into account the nature of the infinite scope of the imagination, afforded to each individual by the fact of consciousness. In this way, dualism is overcome: our finite external (phenomenological) reality does not in any way define or delimit our infinite internal potentiality. Rather, our goal is to transcend the boundaries of the self by engaging with the infinite potentialities of others. We cannot change the structure of "what is" (call it reality or Truth or being), but we can change ourselves and our experience of that structure. That is to say, the only transformation of which we can be certain is an internal one. How is this to be achieved? Bion felt that what he called "the Absolute Truth *about* Ultimate Reality" was to be discovered and explored through the medium of our interaction with others.

Bion appropriated from Freud the notion of the "contact barrier." As he did with all of Freud's insights, Bion

> then uniquely re-conceptualized the contact-barrier as acting like a neuronal "synapse" – that is, functioning as a selectively permeable membrane between the unconscious and consciousness (and the reverse) in order to preserve the integrity and autonomous functioning of each domain so as to permit selective interchange between them.[10]

The threshold between self and other that Bion calls the contact barrier is the realm occupied by silence. By attending to that space, we allow for each person in an interaction to retain integrity and autonomy, and to choose the nature of the interchange that is to follow.

The methodology that we developed prompted us to suspend judgment in the way that we approached our interviewees, attempting to

---

[8] Grotstein, *op. cit.*, 38.
[9] Grotstein, *op. cit.*, 78.
[10] Grotstein, loc. Cit.

set aside the methodological preconceptions of our individual disciplines in order to listen in a more open way. When we speak of suspending judgment, we are attempting to take Bion and Husserl's ideas in a new, interdisciplinary direction. Suspending judgment in this way is by no means a passive process. To the contrary, it is an active and dynamic means by which other forms of judgment can arise for consideration.

For us, the process of ethical silence is a very specific application of the fashionable term "mindfulness." Suspending judgment means listening as an intersubjective presence in the moment. In that instant, we attempt to listen, as well as we can, in the present tense. This requires the listener to apprehend the other in his or her present moment, trying not to superimpose onto the listening one's own history: trying to listen (as far as possible) without a past, without reactivity (e.g., as a result of our own fear, oppression, or shame). It also entails "listening without a future," that is, without pre-emptively anticipating one prospect. Listening in such a way empowers the speaker to choose freely amongst many possibilities or potentialities.

Suspending judgment, then, means attempting to listen to an other without imposing a value bias. Listening to silence properly means suspending dependence or insistence on a particular outcome. If this can be achieved, both the listener and the other can be freed from choosing from amongst a range of previously determined options, so that new and as-yet-unknown options may emerge.

Like the birth of consciousness, the suspension of judgment encompasses both product and process. The reflective nature of silence helps us to hold in abeyance our appraisal of the product and make room to discover what the process is or could be. We believe that the simple act of making space for reflection will result in a more ethical decision because it will entail more consideration of the other.

In our analysis, this space is the wellspring of silence.

Between stimulus and response there is a space. In that space is our power to choose our response. In our response lies our growth and our freedom.[11]

---

[11] This quote is often attributed to Viktor Frankl, but in fact the author is unknown. Frankl was a physician and psychotherapist who survived three years in Nazi concentration camps,

Our research has intensified the conviction that in all cultures and contexts, silence is an important feature of good decision-making and a proven catalyst for transformation. As the foundation of social life, communication is in desperate need of restoration. We believe that a renewed appreciation of the potentialities of silence may offer a path of hope toward a more ethical future. In the midst of the turbulence, noise, and frenzy of these perilous days, we urge you to consider silence anew.

> In the moment before [someone] speaks, language still hovers over the silence it has just left; it hovers between silence and speech. The word is still uncertain where to turn: whether to return wholly into the silence and vanish therein or to make a clear break with silence by becoming a sound. Human freedom decides whither the word shall go... Here, therefore, in the silence one lives between his destruction (since silence can be the beginning of the absolute loss of the word) and his resurrection.[12]

We invite you to choose resurrection of the word, through reflective attention to silence.

REFERENCES

Bion, Francesca. 1995. "The Days of Our Years." In *The Complete Works of W. R. Bion, Volume 15*. London: Karnac Books. Originally published in *The Journal of Melanie Klein and Object Relations*, Vol. 13, no. 1.

Bion, Wilfred. 1976. Penetrating Silence. Presentation to the Study Center for Organizational Leadership and Authority, Los Angeles, California, December 14, 1976. Published in *The Complete Works of W. R. Bion, Volume 15*. London: Karnac Books.

Bion, Wilfred. 1978. "A Seminar in Paris". Transcribed by Francesca Bion. See Jürgen Braungardt, http://braungardt.trialectics.com/sciences/psychoanalysis/bion/seminar-in-paris. Accessed June 5, 2016.

---

including Theresienstadt, Auschwitz, and Dachau. During his captivity, he kept a journal of his reflections and observations, which was eventually published as *Man's Search for Meaning*. Frankl founded a form of psychoanalysis called "logotherapy and existential analysis". The central tenets of this treatment modality are that: (1) humans can exercise free will in response to our experiences; (2) we are free to create meaning from any situation; (3) the creation of purposeful action gives meaning to our lives.

[12] Max Picard, *The World of Silence* (London: Harvill Press), 45 ff.

Bion, Wilfred. 1978. *Seven Servants: "Learning from Experience"; "Elements of Psychoanalysis"; "Transformations"; and "Attention and Interpretation"*. New York: Jason Aronson Inc. Publishers.
Braza, Jerry and Thich Nhat Hahn. 2011. *The Seeds of Love: Growing Mindful Relationships*. North Clarendon, Vermont: Tuttle Publishing.
Brownell, William. 1997. "How the Ear Works: Nature's Solutions for Listening", *Volta Review*, 99(5): 9–28. Accessed October 8, 2016.
Grotstein, James. 2007. *A Beam of Intense Darkness*. London: Karnac Books.
López-Corvo, Rafael. 2003. *The Dictionary of the Work of W. R. Bion*. London: Karnac Books.
Picard, Max. 1952. *The World of Silence*. Trans. by Stanley Godman. London: Harvill Press.
Rilke, Rainer Maria. 1914. "Es winkt zu Fühlung fast aus alle Dingen". *Letzte Gedichte und Fragmentarisches (1910-1926)*. http://www.textlog.de/22437.html. See also http://www.rainer-maria-rilke.de. Accessed October 14, 2016.

INDEX

A

Aboriginal, 24, 96–97, 99–105
Action, 2, 6–11, 13–15, 18–20, 23, 24, 26, 27, 29, 40, 41, 50, 52, 54, 71, 75, 104, 106, 113, 114, 116, 120, 122, 124, 125, 143, 161, 164, 170
Active Listening, 141
Agency, 8, 23, 24, 152
Analysis, 4, 9, 19, 28–32, 34, 37–44, 51–65, 80–91, 98–106, 112–128, 135–145, 151–159, 162, 163, 165, 170, 174
Analyze/analyzing, 2, 5, 17, 18, 31, 57, 75, 100, 103, 136
Artists, 136, 137, 142–144
Attention, 1, 2, 4–8, 11–15, 17–19, 22–24, 27, 29, 31, 41, 43, 49, 71, 75, 76, 103, 104, 112, 127, 141, 142, 161, 163–165, 167–168, 171
Attentive/attentively, 8, 20, 27–28, 73–76, 90, 102, 135, 141, 142, 152, 163, 166
Attitude, 20, 28, 50, 51, 70, 71, 73, 76, 82, 83, 86, 161–167, 171

B

Boundary, 3, 28, 34, 42, 71, 97, 143, 173
Breaking silence, 37, 90

C

Change, 3, 4, 6, 18, 20–25, 30, 63, 81, 85, 98, 99, 102, 106, 112, 115, 119, 124, 125, 128, 139, 162, 169
Child, 13, 14, 19, 39, 43, 63, 70, 72–74, 87, 141, 152, 155
Children, 6, 13, 19, 37, 39, 72, 82, 90, 97, 111, 121, 123
Circumstances, 26, 68, 76, 80, 111, 141, 152
Co-created spaces, 73, 76
Communication/communicated, 1–4, 18, 21, 28, 32, 52, 56, 64, 88, 98, 104–106, 123–124, 151, 158, 161–162, 164, 165, 168–169, 172, 175
Complex/complexity, 1, 3, 25, 27, 29, 32, 86
Comprehend/comprehensive, 2, 29, 31, 142

Conflict, 6, 13, 18, 29, 53, 83, 88, 151
Connection(s), 27, 55, 56, 97, 99, 141, 143, 145, 156, 157
Conscious/consciousness, 6, 7, 10, 11, 14, 18, 20, 21, 23, 39, 41–44, 71, 75, 76, 81–83, 86–88, 104, 106, 121, 122, 128, 137, 143, 145, 161, 163–165, 172–174
Context(s), 1–5, 7, 12, 7, 9, 13, 17, 18, 21, 24, 26, 27, 30, 31, 34, 36–37, 49–51, 56, 58, 61, 68–76, 79–91, 96–98, 101, 104, 106, 109–113, 128, 133–135, 143, 144, 149–152, 156, 161–163, 165, 166, 175
Contextual/contextualization, 18, 28, 30, 31, 42
Culture(s), 20, 26, 41, 44, 51, 52, 59, 71, 76, 82–84, 89, 90, 100, 103, 105, 121, 153, 163, 165, 166, 175

D

Decision-making, 1–4, 17–21, 23–27, 32, 82, 161, 162, 168, 175
Decision(s), 3, 8, 9, 17, 20, 21, 28, 82, 87, 143, 161–164, 168, 170, 171, 174
Dialogue, 20, 22, 27–29, 64, 73, 74, 76, 90, 102, 119, 135, 142–145, 152, 162
Different/differences, 1, 4, 5, 8, 22–23, 28, 30, 50, 60, 61, 64, 70, 76, 89, 97, 99, 102, 120, 152, 157, 165, 168
Differentiation, 9, 11, 164
Dirty War, 36–39
Disability, 67–68, 118

E

Economic(s), 1, 3, 5, 7, 24, 30, 32, 68, 69, 96, 102, 104, 111, 113, 115, 120, 122, 150
Effects, 1, 13, 18, 21, 23, 26–28, 60, 71, 110, 150, 161, 166, 172
Emic, 52, 64, 163
Ethical/ethically, 1–4, 7, 9–11, 17–20, 23, 27, 32, 41, 64, 65, 101, 106, 139, 143, 161–164, 166, 171, 174, 175
Ethics, 1, 3, 5, 8, 9, 12–15, 17–20, 22, 32, 33, 165
Ethnicity, 4, 6, 89
Etic, 49, 52, 64, 65, 163
External, 5, 6, 52, 55, 64, 69, 74, 136, 164, 170, 173

F

Family/families, 2, 24, 37, 38, 40–41, 62, 63, 68, 70–76, 82, 90, 97, 111, 123, 127
Fear(s), 13, 20, 24, 26–27, 37, 41, 59, 61, 62, 73, 76, 85, 90, 102, 120, 122, 123, 141, 152, 153, 159, 165, 168, 172, 174
Features, 1, 4, 5, 125, 151, 168, 170, 175
Five step process, 18
Freedom(s)/freely, 4, 8–10, 12, 15, 22, 27, 29, 76, 82, 87, 97, 117, 151, 172, 174

G

Gender, 38, 49–51, 57, 59, 63, 81, 83, 88, 120, 166
Groups, 2, 4–7, 19, 20, 36, 51, 54, 56, 62, 76, 81, 84, 85, 97–100, 103, 112, 117, 118, 120, 125, 126, 134, 162, 167, 168

H

Healing, 41, 147–159, 167
Humility, 70, 76
Hopelessness/hopeless, 20, 23–24, 61, 62, 72–73, 76, 90, 102, 120, 121, 152, 159
Hope(s)/hoped, 17–19, 23, 26, 28, 31, 32, 34, 41, 73, 76, 85, 98, 152, 161, 164, 167, 175

I

Impact, 3, 5, 76, 96, 98, 104, 112, 115, 145, 166, 172
Implications, 1, 21, 22, 23, 24, 26, 127, 162
In-between spaces, 4, 5, 71, 75, 142, 143
Indigenous, 5–7, 20, 22, 24, 69, 96–100, 106, 149, 165
Individual/individuals, 2–9, 11, 12, 19, 27, 34, 44, 53, 56, 65, 70, 81, 86, 89, 98, 105, 107–128, 143, 151, 163, 167, 168, 170, 172–174
Inform/information, 2, 3, 24, 25, 28, 70, 71, 74, 82, 83, 87, 97, 105, 161, 162, 168
Infusion, 4, 5
Interactions, 6, 12, 17, 18, 20, 21, 25, 28, 29, 34, 64, 70, 71, 74, 76, 86, 90, 101, 104, 106, 112, 127, 139, 165, 166, 171–173
Interdisciplinarity, 3, 28, 33, 34, 164
Interdisciplinary, 1, 3–5, 29, 32–34, 136, 164, 168, 174
Internal, 2, 5–7, 19, 52, 55, 64, 86, 100, 104, 136, 150, 163, 164, 172, 173
Interpret/interpretation, 17, 19, 21, 33, 34, 89, 112, 127, 162
Intersubjective/intersubjectivity, 6–12, 14, 163

K

Knowledge, 9, 25, 26, 28, 29, 43, 85, 87, 97, 100, 105, 106, 139, 165, 168, 171
Known, 10, 19, 37, 94, 109, 133

L

Ladyboy, 49, 57, 62, 63
Layers, 41, 79–91, 162
Learned, 59, 70, 87, 138, 162, 165–170
Levinas, Emmanuel, 7, 9, 10, 12, 15
Linear, 40, 75, 76, 86, 127
Listen/listening, 1, 3, 20, 21, 24, 27–28, 38, 70, 73–76, 90, 102, 103, 135, 141, 142, 152, 159, 165–167, 169, 172, 174

M

Meaning, 5–11, 17, 20, 21, 33, 41, 44, 51, 54, 57, 98, 112, 127, 141, 145, 163, 171
Methodology, 18, 25, 28–34, 40, 152, 164, 165, 167, 168, 174
Misunderstanding, 5, 25, 101, 103
Modalities, 1, 4, 5, 17, 18, 20–33, 58, 61, 64, 72, 73, 76, 89, 101, 102, 112, 127, 128, 135, 141, 142, 151, 152, 155, 162, 163, 165
Modes, 17, 32, 86, 98, 145, 163

N

Noise, 39, 75, 171, 175

O

Oppress/oppression/oppressor, 3, 25, 26, 53, 61, 72–73, 76, 90, 102, 110, 120, 121, 141, 152–154, 159, 162, 174

Oppressed, 20, 24–26
Outsider, 49, 59, 76, 99, 100, 163, 168

P
Philosophy, 1, 3, 7, 15, 32, 33, 125, 171
Plurality, 20, 28, 106
Practitioner, 1, 3, 30–32, 34, 37
Problem/problem solving, 3, 4, 6, 9, 10, 18, 44, 53, 74, 97, 100, 113, 156, 171
Process, 4–7, 25, 27, 39, 40, 54, 56, 58, 63, 74–76, 86, 87, 89, 100, 103, 104, 113, 127, 128, 137, 151, 152, 163–167, 170, 171

R
Recognition, 7, 27, 29, 41, 44, 57, 74, 113, 165, 166, 168
Reflect/reflection, 11, 18, 19, 29–31, 34, 41, 43, 44, 58, 59, 61, 64, 69, 75, 76, 81, 82, 90, 102–104, 112, 123, 128, 137, 161–175
Respond/responsibility, 8, 9, 11, 12, 14, 19, 23–25, 27, 70, 76, 163, 164
Rhetoric, 20–22, 33, 59, 60, 72, 90, 101

S
Scientific, 15, 87
Sex, 49, 51, 57, 58, 61, 62
Sexuality, 51, 59, 118
Silent space, 71, 74, 142, 156
Space(s), 4, 5, 7, 9, 11–12, 20, 22, 28–29, 30, 38, 49, 56, 59, 61, 64, 65, 70, 71–76, 90, 98, 102, 104, 119, 121, 122, 135–139, 142–145, 152, 153, 156, 157, 159, 164–169, 174
Suicides, 2, 90–91

T
Thinking, 5, 6, 18, 21, 22, 25, 27, 28, 29, 34, 39, 44, 54, 56, 71, 73, 75, 76, 87, 93, 103, 104, 121, 128, 136, 137, 140, 141, 145, 164, 169, 173
Threshold, 6, 11, 14, 59, 138–139, 143, 168–169, 173
Time, 25, 52, 56, 58, 59, 74, 88, 97, 99, 110, 111, 124, 128, 135, 140, 156, 163, 166, 168
Tools, 29, 136, 139
Tradition/traditional/traditionally, 7, 20, 24, 28, 36, 37, 51, 52, 81–85, 87, 89, 96, 97, 101, 121, 149, 165, 168
Transform/transformation/transformative, 1, 6, 20, 21, 25, 27, 32, 41, 44, 50, 56, 63, 64, 106, 124, 139, 173, 175
Trauma, 35, 37, 38, 41, 43, 60, 61, 98, 162, 168
Tribal, 76, 82, 87, 96, 98, 149, 153
Trust, 25, 27, 56, 59, 62, 75, 86, 106

U
Unknown/unknowable, 67–77, 165, 167, 173, 174

V
Violence, 2, 39, 43, 57–63, 90, 118, 121, 124, 125, 150, 153, 154, 156

Violent, 124, 152, 159
Voice, 2–3, 17–19, 23–26, 28, 30, 33, 34, 42–43, 49, 55, 73, 74, 76, 81, 82, 88–91, 119–120, 153, 155, 162, 171

W

Weil, Simone, 7, 8, 11, 15

Western, 7, 69, 81, 82, 86, 87, 117
Willing/willingness, 22, 23, 70, 76, 139
Winnicott, Donald, 13, 14
Wojtyla, Karol, 10
Women, 36–39, 50, 51, 57, 82, 84–87, 90, 111, 117, 119–120, 151, 158

The manufacturer's authorised representative in the EU is Springer Nature Customer Service Centre GmbH, Europaplatz 3, 69115 Heidelberg, Germany. If you have any concerns regarding our products, please contact ProductSafety@springernature.com

Printed and bound by CPI Group (UK) Ltd, Croydon, CR0 4YY
23/03/2026
02076683-0001